A Sense
of the Sacred

A Sense
of the Sacred

A Biography of Bede Griffiths

KATHRYN SPINK

ORBIS BOOKS

Maryknoll, New York 10545

The Catholic Foreign Mission Society of America (Maryknoll) recruits and trains
people for overseas missionary service. Through Orbis Books, Maryknoll aims to
foster the international dialogue that is essential to mission. The books published,
however, reflect the opinions of their authors and are not meant to represent the
official position of the society.

First published in the United Kingdom by SPCK, Holy Trinity Church, Marylebone
Road, London NW1 4DU, UK. © Kathryn Spink 1988

United States edition published 1989 by Orbis Books, Maryknoll, NY 10545

Typeset in Great Britain and printed and bound in the United States of America

Library of Congress Cataloging-in-Publication Data

Spink, Kathryn.
  A sense of the sacred.

  Bibliography: p.
  Includes index.
  1. Griffiths, Bede, 1906-   . 2. Benedictines—
Biography.   I. Title.
BX4705.G6226S64   1988   271'.1'024   [B]   88-15270
ISBN 0-88344-442-9

For Hazel Nash

Contents

Acknowledgements

A special debt of gratitude is owed to Father Bede who gave so generously of his time and energy in the preparation of this book and who authorized the use of all his own writings. The author would also like to express her thanks to the community at Saccidananda Ashram, to Barbara Griffiths, Abbot Dyfrig Rushton OSB, Martyn Skinner, Dorothea Pickering, to Wolfgang Somary, Hillary Wackman, Tony Mendonca, to Freddie Bose of Kashmir Holidays, to Es and Shirley Fonseca, and to the many other friends and fellow-travellers who helped to make this book possible. Thanks are also due to Derek Blew for permission to use the photographs reproduced on pp. 4 (top) 5 (top) and 8 of the illustrated section of this book.

Return to India

In a way the journey really began in the great mountain silence of rock and stream and scrub and snow. I had returned to India, to the Himalayas where just over thirty years previously I had been born. In some very secret way this land, my birthplace, had been calling to me for years. Like so many others who journeyed from the West to Tibet, Japan or India I had come there in response to vague and indeterminate yearnings, but I had come too in the dim awareness that my real destination lay not so very many physical miles away, and that the long hours of travel that separated England from the East were but the expression of an inner distance. Yet for a while, on arrival, I could perceive only those elements that emphasized the cultural, the physical divide, and I found myself hopelessly out of step with the land that once had seemed my 'home'. Only in the fierce clarity of the mountain air, in the transforming silence with its genius of giving back to itself, was a certain vision restored; and even then my impressions were, I knew, subjective, the observations of one whose direct experience of India was limited yet whose indirect links with the country had engendered certain expectations and who had come in readiness to have those expectations confirmed. The purpose of the route through India, some thirty years after Fr Bede Griffiths had first set foot in the land which had been for him also the focal point of deep-rooted aspirations, was to place his life and message in a contemporary Indian context. India, increasingly subject to the materialistic and sceptical influences of the West, had undoubtedly changed since first Father Bede had asked himself the question whether the spiritual tradition of India could withstand the shock of western materialism. A gulf of years, intellect, insight and a multitude of other factors separated his arrival by boat in Bombay from my own landing at New Delhi airport and it was only later, much later, that I would be able to discern the common elements in our respective experiences or at least to see that mine were not without a certain relevance to his.

The first week in India left me battered, confused and exhausted. Together with my husband, who had joined me for a month of my stay, I had spent several days of frenetic activity in Delhi, visiting friends and exploring what our well intentioned taxi-driver considered to be the essential tourist attractions. They were many and impressive. We had marvelled at the still splendid manifestations of past pomp and power, we had stepped gingerly, shoes in hand, across the courtyards of the capital's mosques, and we had watched not without a certain cynicism but nonetheless intrigued as a young man in the shadow of the great walls of the Red Fort stretched out on the ground beneath a scarlet blanket then proceeded to levitate his still horizontal body twenty feet into the air. We had clung warily to our cameras and our purses as we toured well-kept formal gardens and admired the bulbous domes, the red and white sandstone and the marble of Moghul-style tombs with their high arched entrances beneath which bees nested un-disturbed and noisy in the heat. We had struggled breathlessly through the colour and congestion of the bazaars and survived our first encounters with the country's poverty: the lepers' stumps thrust close to our faces to reinforce the urgency of a request for *paisa*, the constant noisy pressure to give and to buy and, most heartrending of all, the silent presence of the sick and the hungry who, too weak to beg, huddled, heads bowed and unobtrusive on the street corners. Finally, aware that this was but a homeopathic dose of things to come we had retreated, relieved, guilty and with a profound sense of personal in-adequacy to a hotel garden where the scent of orange blossom obscured the city smells, parrots flitted through the trees and waiters dressed in white tunics and orange cummerbunds and turbans padded soft-footed between the restaurant tables.

There had been other moments of respite: the warmth and hospitality of Indian hosts, moments snatched in the Raj Ghat, the park on the banks of the Yamuna river where a simple square platform of black marble marks the spot where Mahatma Gandhi was cremated. Nearby, in the shade of a stone archway a bearded Indian swathed in a *khadi* loincloth sat spinning with a wheel as Gandhi had daily spun on his ashram. About him there had been a concentration and serenity which communicated itself as he enquired from what country we came and explained the full significance of his wheel, an inner peace which seemed to signal an India far removed from the traffic jams and city suits of New Delhi, an India into which western technology with all its benefits and its corresponding evils had not as yet intruded too destructively, that other India in search of which so many of the young Westerners, often dressed in Indian clothes, had come.

Children of a television culture, they had also come in quest of powerful and first-hand experiences. One traveller, asleep in the heat of an afternoon beside a deserted road, finding himself rudely woken by a cobra swaying in response to its charmer's pipe, had curbed his irritation with precisely that thought. He had come to India for novel experiences and having his slumbers disrupted by an importunate reptile was simply one of these. There would be countless others, for India is somehow very powerfully present, at least to those who venture there from places where tradition, character and culture have spread the curtailing influence of reserve over spontaneity. The noise, colour and bursting vitality of religious processions into which throngs of Hindus, Jains and members of a multitude of other sects would merge irrespective of the diversity of their individual beliefs; the eerie shadows cast in the early morning emptiness of the streets of Old Delhi by the rickshaw wallahs draped across the seats of their ramshackle vehicles and the pavement dwellers surfacing from their improvised shelters to confront the heat and the fumes of the day; the sea of upturned smiling faces and outstretched arms of the orphaned and abandoned children in the care of Mother Teresa's Missionaries of Charity; these and a multitude of other vivid impressions seemed to signal that we had entered a world which called for the surrender of reason, a world where nothing was really extraordinary or quite impossible or inconsistent. It was an impression which our Hindu taxi-driver in Delhi was happy to endorse. He stood beside us in the Sisters' compound in an unmistakable attitude of reverence while we delivered medicines and letters from England to Mother Teresa. For him that day had brought an unexpected blessing. The mere proximity of one whose holiness he did not fail to recognize meant a *darshan*. He did not in the least mind waiting, he informed us, because we were on 'a very good mission'. He was courteous, full of admiration for the work of the Missionaries of Charity and devout, none of which prevented him from making his purely financial motives for adopting us for the entire duration of our stay in Delhi unequivocally clear.

It was not long before we discovered that the desire to demonstrate that nothing was impossible frequently entailed saying 'yes', or at least responding with a wonderfully ambiguous wag of the head, to requests well known to be incapable of implementation. The image of the taxi-driver squeezing his vehicle at breakneck speed into an impossible gap between a number of ambling cows and a rapidly oncoming bus with passengers spilling out of the windows, to the cry of, 'It's no problem', had become a popular cartoon among European travellers. In such an atmosphere small achievements assume the dimensions of the miraculous, and it was in this light that we came to regard the way in which our London bookings spanned the intervening distance and translated themselves into carefully pencilled notes bearing close approximations of our names fluttering outside the dusty carriages of Indian trains; but then perhaps there was indeed something miraculous about such an achievement and perhaps it was significant that it had taken the air of India, the apparent chaos of Indian railway stations and their maelstrom of life to awaken us to the fact.

We had opted to travel 'first class' and there had been a certain unease attached to that option just as there had been to our selection of five-star hotels for the initial stages of the journey. Our purpose in travelling in the first place had been an attempt to experience as much as we could of Indian life within the short space of time available to us and not to remove ourselves from it, but we had justified our choice in terms of the need to remain healthy and fit to work, and there were many occasions during the ensuing weeks when, despite our admiration for the Indian people who could travel 'third class', in congestion so dense it was impossible even to count the numbers to a compartment, sleep in virtually any position and remain cheerful and even-tempered throughout, we were glad to indulge our own relative frailty. In any case 'first class' in India was not quite all that the expression might suggest to the cosseted western mind. Our compartment on the first train journey from Delhi to the foothills of the Himalayas contained two wooden bunks, one up, one down, a cracked mirror, two small shelves and a fan which functioned only intermittently, all of which were covered in a thick layer of grime guaranteed to destroy all whimsical notions about travel in steam trains. The window was equipped with both bars and sturdy shutters, the door was studded with heavy bolts and no sooner had we landed our luggage on board than a kindly guard appeared and instructed us, for our own protection, to lock ourselves in and not to open the shutters or doors to anyone.

It was a night of painful introduction to a simpler life, interspersed with the cries of the succession of vendors who walked the length of the train and back again with their kettles full of milky sweetened tea, their barrows of fruit and their trays of sweetmeats, each time it halted at one of the many stations. But then, in the very early morning, glimpsed through blackened shutters, there were the blue-green foothills, the flowering rhododendrons and the long wastes of shining sand and shingle that at other times of the year were awash with melted snow. Six thousand feet up and some fifteen miles beyond the end of the railway track was what had been described as Mussoorie's most prestigious hotel. Constructed for the most part out of wood and once resplendent when in the time of the Raj it had become fashionable to retreat from the heat of the plains, now many of its imposing suites were in a dangerous state of disintegration. The dirt on the windows, cupboards and grand piano in the vast dining hall spoke of long periods of disuse, but the crumbling balconies looked out towards the snow-capped peaks that formed the boundary with China, and the fact that there were only five guests in the hotel focused attention on what might otherwise have been missed. It was impossible accurately to guess the age of the grey-haired, bandy-legged head waiter who picked his way through the endless array of tables that separated the one at which he insisted on seating us from the serving hatch, but he had worked in the hotel for over forty years and he served us curry, the same mutton curry that would reappear each evening for five days, with meticulous correctness. He was a mountain man and one for whom the superhuman peaks amongst which he had been born and raised represented the point at which the eternal entered into time. He walked the laborious route between the shabby tables as if paving his road to immortality and nothing, not even the stains on his maroon tunic and Gandhi cap, could detract from the dignity that his conviction gave him. One evening, towards the end of our stay, as he stood respectfully with his hands behind his back while we finished the inevitable mutton curry, he talked a little of his life. Finally, he raised his hands palm upwards to the heavens then brought them together in the Hindu gesture of salutation: 'Sahib, Memsahib,' he bowed to each of us in turn, 'May your union and your journey be blessed.' To him, or so it appeared to me, his journey, our journey, every journey, was potentially a pilgrimage towards a greater understanding of God. The philosophy of his life found its tangible expression in the temples which perched precariously on Himalayan peaks seemingly to test the devotion of those who made the arduous climb to worship there.

The very unexpectedness of the old man's benediction

brought with it a sense of having arrived at last in the India I was seeking. The search was more in a spirit of abstract enquiry than active participation but its objective remained very clear: a place where the sense of the immanence of God prevailed. Next morning, we climbed a further 2,000 feet into the mountains to visit the Surkhanda Devi temple, a journey which involved scrambling the last half mile on foot. Struggling, breathless and gasping in the thin air, it was impossible not to admire the dedication of the Hindu pilgrims from the plains as they too wheezed their way up the narrow, steeply sloping track in the conviction that the more difficulty they experienced in attaining the place of worship, the more potent was their act of devotion. The temple itself consisted of an open expanse of grass on the very tip of the rocky mound with an enclosed shrine and a large bell at either end. When at last we reached it, our fellow climbers each in turn rang one or other of the bells to waken the god and alert him to their presence, removed their shoes to walk upon the central expanse of grass and spent a few moments in the darkened sanctuary into which we were not permitted to enter. 'Dark', explained one of the temple Brahmins, 'because God is mysterious, as mysterious as the sky.' He waved his arm in an expansive gesture at the snow-covered mountains rolling away into the distance as far as the eye could see and at the burnished sky above. The place, the spectacle and that vast immutable silence all proclaimed the sky as no purely material thing.

During those days spent among the hilltops, briefly pink at sunset but ofen veiled in mist, the tiny hovels and the small pockets of maize cultivated with wooden ploughs drawn by cattle moving at precarious angles on impossibly steep slopes, the patches of pine forest clinging to the rockface and the rushing torrents of life-giving water, we caught a glimpse of the sense of the presence of God in nature and the soul, the kind of natural mysticism which forms the basis of so much of Indian spirituality. For the shy but overwhelmingly friendly mountain people God was immanent. Not for them the tendency of some Christians to concentrate upon the transcendence of a God high above. For them, as for Hindus in general, God was immanent in all created things – in the earth, in water, in fire, in the air, in plants, in animals and in people. Such a view, though deeply Christian also, had, it seemed to us then, been lost to the West to some degree. It was one inevitably much more easily rediscovered in places of great natural beauty among people of incomparable charm. Watching from train windows as we rattled our way through Rajasthan from Jaipur to Agra and on to the 'eternal' city of Varanasi, or Benares, we came to respect the way in which in the early hours of the morning Indian businessmen on the way to work in the towns would get out of the trains at a suitable station dressed in their *dhotis*, produce from their briefcases neatly folded trousers, shirts and ties, and proceed to change discreetly and wash at the water tap always available on the platform. Even these very improvised washes were apparently sacred, undertaken in the awareness that the water comes down from heaven, is received on the head of Shiva, the great god, who distributes it through all the rivers of the earth. The water is therefore received by the more devout Hindu with gratitude to God who provides it.

Despite the influences of Marxism and western humanism, the sense of religion is still strong in India. Millions of people go on pilgrimage each year to the sacred shrines. While we were still in the North preparations were being made for the Kumbh Mela at Hardwar which draws as many as half a million people to a location considered especially propitious because here at the base of the Sawalik Hills the sacred Ganges River leaves the Himalayas and enters into the plains. Everywhere in India there are sacred places, sacred hills, sacred streams, sacred trees. In the most sophisticated shops and offices it is by no means rare to find joss-sticks burning before the brightly coloured image of some tutelary god. Small boys with ragged clothes and no shoes touting for their fathers' businesses would speak of how they dreamt of one day being wealthy men, but then would add with calm acceptance 'but only if God wills it'. Each and every rickshaw wallah we encountered had his own philosophy in which the

8

will of God was given free expression and each as we rode past the statue of one or other of the multitude of gods in the Hindu pantheon would be eager to explain its significance. Often they would explain too that the gods and goddesses were the names and forms of the one nameless and formless Being. A more educated Hindu guide in Sarnath, the place to which the Buddha came to preach his message of the middle way, referred to a quotation from the *Rig-Veda*, *Ekam sat vipra bahuda vadanti* – 'the one Being the wise call by many names'. Hinduism, he was at pains to elaborate, was not a polytheistic religion, for polytheism meant the worship of the many apart from the One, whereas traditional doctrine taught that there was but one infinite Being of which all the gods and goddesses were forms and manifestations. The worship of instructed Hindus was invariably directed towards that 'one Being' and the insight that the numerous gods and goddesses were forms and manifestations of the One was something which, with time we would discover, even the villager today possesses. Yet to the uninitiated eye India seemed constantly to waver between polytheism (even idolatry, for the statues of the divinities were washed in milk, decorated and carried in procession), monotheism and pantheism which held that beyond everything was a divine impersonality which was the same in God, in man and in the world and in which everything must ultimately be absorbed.

Furthermore, even accepting that the one God expresses himself in everything meant coming to terms with the fact that to the Indians God is as much in selling sweetmeats, cleaning your teeth or taking a rickshaw ride as in bathing in the Ganges or silent meditation. It meant perceiving a sense of the sacred in the noise and bustle and seeming irreverence of the busier places of worship in Delhi, Jaipur or Varanasi as well as in the contemplation of the mountain holy men who sat unmoving in isolated places and so evidently sought the one Being in the cave of their own hearts. It was this very anomaly of the Brahmin meditating in the forest and in the town a few miles away temple prostitution, cruelty and monstrosity which had induced C.S. Lewis to see Hinduism not so much as a philosophical maturity of Paganism but as a 'mere oil-and-water coexistence of philosophy side by side with Paganism unpurged'.

Long before we reached Varanasi we had been warned to expect a shock. 'One big slum', was how a Dutch visitor who had come to this place of Hindu pilgrimage expecting a more western atmosphere of sanctity had described it. He had retreated hastily. So much noise, so much life: the streets of the 'city of Shiva' were packed with cycle and motorized rickshaws, old dilapidated cars, wandering cows, buffalo, pilgrims, vendors of every conceivable commodity, beggars, holy men clad only 'in the sky' and people who had come to spend their last days on the banks of the sacred river because it is considered especially auspicious to die here, ensuring instant liberation from the series of births and deaths that *karma* might otherwise ordain to be necessary before salvation is achieved. It was almost impossible to struggle through the milling throngs to the ghats which line the west bank of the Ganges. The steps which led down to the water, from which the pilgrims make their entry into the river, smelt strongly of urine, from a number of buildings along the riverbank there blared a strange cacophony of sound, and we were instantly commandeered by a boy who professed to be still at school and eager to practise his English but who, it later transpired, was in fact a tout for one of the many silk businesses in Varanasi. His actual role was to lure unsuspecting foreigners via a 'free' conducted tour of the ghats, the temples and the shrines to a house in a narrow backstreet from which his employer conducted his business. Accustomed by this time to such practices, we were led against our better judgement, the conscious victims of his ingenuity and powers of persuasion, past women bathing discreetly in their saris, men in extraordinary yoga positions, Brahmin priests sheltering beneath umbrellas from the afternoon sun and offering blessings for a price, and the omnipresent beggars providing others with the opportunity to improve their *karma*.

As we approached Manikarnika, the principle burning ghat

where the bodies of the dead are cremated before their ashes are scattered on the Ganges, our self-appointed guide warned us to put away our cameras. Such cremations, he advised us, were sacred and not a suitable subject for photography. It was a view which we were more than happy to respect. We watched from a distance, with admiration for the calm serenity of the mourners, as an eldest son walked five times round his father's funeral pyre before setting light to it. Then, as the clouds of smoke scented with sandalwood rose into the air, Pappu's whispering voice informed us that the ghat attendants would be prepared to let us photograph the funeral rites for a fee. When we showed no interest the voice became more pressing. The family of the deceased was poor. A proportion of the money we paid would go towards the cost of the funeral which they could ill afford. If we gave the money to the ghat attendant, he would stand beside us while the photograph was taken and the mourners would know that we had made a donation towards their costs and not be offended. Stressing that the bulk of the money must go to the bereaved family and not without a certain uneasiness, we paid the attendant and took the photograph. Below us, up to his waist in water, a man with a basket was sifting the Ganges. The member of a low caste, 'the same as that of the people who clean the town', he was searching for gold, the nose rings and other ornaments which were sometimes tipped into the river with the ashes, which he would then surrender to the owner of the ghat, 'a very, very wealthy man'. 'Do not think you have given much' was the parting shot of the ghat attendant. His words found a more painful resonance in us than perhaps even he suspected.

Like our Dutch friend who had found the whole atmosphere of Varanasi quite extraordinary, with its ghats each adorned with a lingam of Shiva and its temples, often rich in the most explicit sexual imagery, in which monkeys might frolic unimpeded but near which no foreign visitor could venture without the onslaught of Brahmins exploiting every conceivable means of extracting money, we too might have retreated had it not been for a prearranged itinerary. It was all a very far cry from the cathedrals and churches of England, the soft drone of cultured voices, but we stayed and we understood. We understood that India had not cut off God from life. At dawn the hundred or more ghats constructed on the west bank of the Ganges so that they could face the sun rising over the open expanse of countryside to the east were enveloped in a tranquil almost magical atmosphere. Viewed from a boat rowed noiselessly down the sacred river, the Brahmins seated in attitudes of contemplation beneath their umbrellas, the small girls proffering candles on miniature rafts of flowers and the bathers with their receptacles in which afterwards they would take Ganges water to the Golden Temple were as attractive and as welcome to us as the exotically fragrant flower stalls we would sometimes chance upon just when the smell of the drains and the hot cooking fat was most overpowering in the narrow alleyways of India's bazaars. It no longer seemed to matter that only yards from the pilgrim bathers the *dhobi-wallahs* were 'breaking the rocks with the washing'.

We understood, too, that the sexual symbolism which so pervades Hinduism was deeply significant: God so created the world that everything is a play of the union of the male and the female, of the active and the passive principles. This is the mystery of creation. Properly understood, the lingam of Shiva found on every ghat in Shiva's city and so prevalent elsewhere, need not be obscene. Rather it represented not only the 'source of life' but also the absolute 'formless divinity', the stone scarcely shaped in contrast with the rich profusion of imagery elsewhere. For Hinduism is steeped in imagery and symbolism. The water tank we frequently encountered at the entrance to Hindu temples in the course of our travels was, we discovered, for purgative washing. The worshipper entering the temple must first cleanse himself from sin. The breaking of a coconut before the shrine of Ganesh, the elephant-headed god with the power to remove obstacles was a particularly meaningful part of his devotions. The hard, rough shell represents the external self, the ego; the sweet white milk inside symbolizes the divine life within. The breaking of the shell before the shrine of Ganesh is thus a breaking of the ego, the attempt to remove all the obstacles from the mind and make it open to God. By visiting all the courts of the temple and the many shrines of the different gods the worshipper relates himself to all the cosmic powers they represent in an endeavour to bring himself into harmony with the universe. This represents the illuminative way, the path of God revealing himself in the cosmos. Finally, there is the *garbha griha*, the 'house of the womb', the source of life, the inner sanctuary which is always dark because God, the ultimate mystery, dwells in darkness, beyond the light of this world.

In a sense the Hindu temple is itself essentially a sacrament, a representation of the divine mystery manifested in nature and the human soul. The outer walls often depict the world of nature, of plants and animals and men gradually rising to the world of the gods. The approach to the inner shrine involves a progression through various stages of purification before the *garbha griha* is reached, the holy place which is the centre both of the universe and of the soul, simultaneously the 'womb' from which all things spring and the 'cave within the heart' where man enters into communion with the ultimate mystery. These were but some illustrations among many of the richness of meaning in Hindu worship.

Pujas or acts of worship, whether performed in vast temples with many *pujaris* or in tiny villages throughout India followed the same basic form. First, food, the fruit of the earth, is placed on a leaf then it is purified with an offering of water which is sprinkled round it. Next, incense in a bowl is waved over the offering in a process called *arati* which signifies the offering of air. Then camphor is burnt, signifying the offering of fire. Camphor is used because it burns with a pure flame: it leaves no residue and thus symbolizes the soul burning itself out in the service of God. This too is waved round the offering. Thus the four elements – earth, water, air and fire are offered to God as a sign of the offering of all creation in sacrifice. Some of this insight I would acquire during my stay at the ashram or hermitage for which I was ultimately bound. Some was gleaned from a corpulent Brahmin seated beneath a pillar in a courtyard adjacent to the Golden Temple in Varanasi. He was wise and friendly, his English was broken but readily comprehensible and seated alone in his presence it came to me, not for the first time, that contact with Hinduism at its deepest level must surely teach Christianity a deeper sense of its own mystery.

When we had finished speaking my companion picked up a garland of golden marigolds from a number he had beside him and made to put it round my neck. Seeing the bowl of small coins in front of him and not having any money with me, I tried to decline graciously. By this time I had grown accustomed to the idea that nothing was given gratuitously to 'sahibs' and 'memsahibs'. Still the Brahmin held out the marigolds and eventually I was compelled to explain that I had no money to give him. A flicker of surprise passed over his face rapidly followed by an expression of unmistakable sympathy. The garland of marigolds was placed firmly round my neck with a gesture that I must keep it free of any charge. Guilt-stricken at my own cynicism, I gave the generous Brahmin the plastic ballpoint pen I had been using to take notes and hurried back to our hotel.

Once again India had toppled our preconceptions. There remained nonetheless the feeling that while Hinduism was based on a deeply mystical experience and everywhere sought to experience the reality of God in the depths of the soul, it was perhaps for that very reason an extremely individualistic religion. Each one goes to God in his own way. Even when a family visited a temple together each individual, it seemed, was worshipping by himself. The temple is not, like a Christian church, a place for the assembly for shared worship. Hinduism is not, like Christianity, a community religion; and perhaps it was as an extension of this lack of a sense of corporate unity that, despite the indisputable generosity of many Hindus, the commitment to caring for one's fellow man did not appear to be as powerfully present. The same educated travel representative who was quick to push painfully thin and struggling porters almost brutally out of the way would smile upon a cow wandering along the railway track and obstructing the passage of the oncoming trains: 'It's a free country.' Indeed, the respect for life in its animal form was impressive in its consequences. It goes without saying that the sacred cows could wander freely without fear of harm. In Jaipur where their presence seemed particularly prominent it was explained that, despite appearances to the contrary, they nearly all belonged to somebody. Because their owners had no land on which to put them out to graze, they let them roam loose, tempting them back to be milked at a given point each day with something special for them to eat. When they ceased to provide milk their owners simply turned them loose altogether, secure in the knowledge that no one would ever harm them. It was not, however, only cows which were afforded such kindness. The relationship with buffalo, camels, horses, birds, all forms of animal life was an easy and rarely aggressive one with the result that the creatures themselves were approachable, even tame. Birds would descend upon open-air restaurant tables and peck at the food on the plates undeterred by the presence of the human diners. Yet people could suffer on the streets without causing the passers-by so much as to stop and look.

It was a long established and much recognized hiatus. The explanations offered to account for it were familiar ones: *karma*, self preservation, the impossibility of any individual confronting an issue as enormous as that of India's poor, national pride which would not allow the acknowledgement of such a problem. For me, the reason why a taxi-driver would with infinite care remove some rather venomous looking insect from his vehicle and set it free with evident satisfaction yet look with nothing but a kind of disdainful embarrassment at the people of the slums, remained a mystery. Why was it that the love of God did not transform itself into concern, a word which Mother Teresa has defined as 'the practical expression of God's love'? The fact remained that often it seemed to be Mother Teresa and the many unsung Christian 'saints' like her, who in Calcutta and in places of extreme need elsewhere provided the real impetus for charity at an individual level. Mother Teresa herself maintains that she and her Sisters and Brothers would be unable to undertake the service that they do, were it not for the conviction that in cleansing the maggot-ridden wounds of the dying they are actually tending the wounds of the suffering Christ. No other motivation but their Christian faith, she insists, would make such arduous and such filthy work possible.

In the two long rooms that once served as a rest home for pilgrims to the Kali temple in Calcutta but which are now *Nirmal Hriday*, the Home for the Dying run by Missionaries of Charity, we were brought to a new appreciation of her words. In order really to understand poverty, she has said, you have to touch it. Touching the broken bodies, so emaciated that their bones dug painfully into the thin mattresses arranged in rows on either side of the two rooms, was a moving and a humbling experience. For a while it was no longer possible to deal in reasoned abstractions or merely to observe as they suffered without bitterness or protest and with such extraordinary dignity. The same Spirit that stirred in them stirred in us. We cut their hair and nails, held them in our arms and helped to turn them over when the voluntary medical helpers needed to examine otherwise inaccessible wounds. Christian faith at its most articulate, in action, had attracted numerous helpers. That day alone in *Nirmal Hriday* there were medical helpers from the United States, Australia and England, and other volunteers, European and Indian, to help clean, run errands and generally to care. Among these, serving food to the 'untouchables', was a high caste Hindu lady, one of many, we were given to understand, who help the Sisters in their work.

Calcutta, a city where so many of the destitute have lived out their shortened lives and died beneath the stars, is an extraordinary place, extraordinary for the magnitude of its need and for the response that need evokes in people. We saw the long queues of poor people waiting for their rations of milk powder and bulgar outside the walls of *Prem Dan*, the home in which the Missionaries of Charity also care for the sick and the mentally handicapped. We visited the Loreto

Sisters' school for orphans and children with only one parent and the home for the otherwise homeless elderly run by the Little Sisters of the Poor. We drove out of the city to *Udayan*, the home of the Resurrection where an Englishman, James Stevens, and his team provide accommodation, schooling and training in skills such as tailoring for the children of lepers. Once the owner of a prosperous business in England, James had initiated *Udayan* by one day driving a truck into the slums and offering the children of the most ostracized of all outcastes the hope of a better future. Everywhere we turned in Calcutta there seemed to be people working selflessly for others with exceptional courage and exceptional joy. There was the joy too, the indomitable spirit, of so many of the poor themselves, of the children who derived such happiness from toys improvised from sticks, bits of paper or scrap, of the people scouring the city's rubbish heaps for anything they might use or sell, of the 'human horses' struggling to pull overweight *marwari* businessmen through the city's hazardous streets in hand-drawn rickshaws, of those who were prepared literally to sell their blood in order that their families might eat, and who managed miraculously to smile throughout. Among them there was not the same lack of concern. They knew how to share the little that they had, to care for their families and for others whose lot was as arduous as their own, and, stripped and broken as they were, how to put their trust in the grace of God. There was much that the materially poor of India could teach the spiritually poor of the West.

In the Home for the Dying, the poor, Mother Teresa has said, die 'like angels'. Emerging from *Nirmal Hriday* where the unaccountably peaceful atmosphere reflects the serenity of its inmates, into the hubbub of the approach to the Kali temple was not an easy transition. Amongst the stalls laden with flowers and the succession of small shrines and images we came upon an enclosed area stained with the blood of past sacrifices. A trembling, terrified goat was about to be slaughtered. Suddenly we were confronted with the dark side of Hinduism. The only Europeans surrounded by a sea of faces in which we began to discern traces of hostility, we withdrew hastily. The rumours of human sacrifices carried out in the Amber Palace near Jaipur no longer seemed quite so inconceivable. Certainly, it was no longer difficult to imagine the opposition that Mother Teresa had encountered when first she had endeavoured to provide a place in which the suffering people of the streets could die with dignity, having experienced what it was to be loved. She had been accused of attempting to convert the poor to Christianity at the very heart of Hinduism. Outside the former pilgrims' rest home an angry crowd had gathered and thrown stones at the tiny woman who has always insisted that Hindus and Moslems who die in the care of the Missionaries of Charity should be able to do so according to the rituals of their faith. Water from the Ganges is sprinkled on the lips of dying Hindus; Moslems are read passages from the Koran. The avowed intention behind all the work of the Missionaries of Charity is not to convert to Christianity but to make a Hindu a better Hindu, a Moslem a better Moslem and so on. Yet it has at times provoked hostile and even violent reactions from a people who pride themselves on a religious tolerance based on the view that all religions are but different paths to the one goal: *moksha*, liberation, which may be attained in this world, and must be attained eventually by all beings in the course of rebirth.

Calcutta had in some way brought to a head the powerful reactions which India as a whole evoked, for India reacts very strongly on people. Some love it, some loathe it, most do both. I found myself caught up in a constant state of ambivalence, loving India for its beauty, for the warmth, spontaneity and insight of its people, yet repelled by its ugliness and filth, the deviousness of the many whose capacity for trickery knew no bounds and their apparent callousness which seemed strangely compatible with great generosity of heart. Madras confirmed these feelings. The south of India appeared, at least to us, in some way softer than the north. The taxi-drivers and rickshaw cyclists were less pushing. There were fewer beggars. The streets of Madras were cleaner than those of Calcutta. But there were slums in Madras too and there were the same apparent inconsistencies. Early one morning we visited Kapaleeschwara Temple, an ancient Shiva temple with an imposing *gopuram*. Officially, as with many other functioning temples in Tamil Nadu, non-Hindus were allowed only into the outer courtyard but we were instantly approached by a young man who offered in return for a fee to take us further inside. Weary of such approaches and uncertain in any case of his authority to waive the rules on our behalf, we elected instead to view the *gopuram* from the steps of the man-made 'lake' outside. In it a number of people were engaged in ritual bathing, deeply absorbed in cleansing themselves before entering the temple. Yet the steps which ran down to the water on all four sides of this sizeable tank were studded with piles of human excrement. The stench in the heat was overwhelming. Doubtless there were good reasons why people were reduced to using a place of ritual bathing as a vast lavatory, but the close association of cleanliness and godliness was too deeply ingrained in us for us not to feel a certain disgust. We took refuge in the nearby San Thomé Cathedral, a doubtless incongruously western building said to house the remains of St Thomas, but a welcome haven of hygiene in which to struggle with our conditioning.

For me, the ambivalence of the feelings that India inspired would find their clearest expression some time later when alone in Tiruchirappalli I clambered aboard a bus to visit the Srirangam – Sri Ranganathaswamy temple complex. Probably the largest temple complex in India, it has twenty-one *gopurams* altogether and seven concentric walls. Non-Hindus may not, of course, enter the innermost sanctuary but they may otherwise wander freely from shrine to shrine. I made my way through the bazaars, Brahmins' houses and barbers' shops that occupied the space between the outer four walls only to be joined as I walked by a succession of young men, each professing to be the 'official' guide to the temple and proclaiming loudly that the others were not. At the fourth wall visitors were required to remove their shoes. A number of shoe minders materialized as if out of thin air. For a small fee it was possible to climb on top of the wall to look over the complex. Touts bore down on me from the 'Art Gallery' in which the tickets were sold. If I wished to take a camera with me there would be an additional charge. Hands were already outstretched to receive the money. It was May and in the south of India the temperature was rising with each passing day. There were times when the sky itself seemed almost white hot. I had spent the morning in the Indian Airlines office trying to confirm my return flight to Madras with an official who smiled beguilingly, offered me tea and did precisely nothing; and I had come to the temple in search of peace and respite. Finally, I turned on my entourage and explained calmly but with all the firmness I could muster that whilst I appreciated that without the benefit of their extensive knowledge my understanding of the fine carvings and numerous shrines would be limited, on this occasion at least I would like to view them on my own. Surprisingly, they retreated, but something of my desperation must have continued to be apparent as I wandered alone through the gateway in the third wall. In the shade of a great pillar a woman was lying snoozing in the midday heat. Seeing me, she beckoned and patted the ground beside her. As I hesitated, she repeated the action, so I sat down beside her at the foot of the column. She spoke no English; I spoke no Tamil but she smiled her reassurance then closed her eyes again, her hand still resting on my arm. A few moments later a beautiful young girl in a golden yellow sari tapped me gently on the shoulder. She, too, smiled before murmuring a few words which I could not understand and placing two bananas in my lap. Always such gestures of spontaneous warmth and generosity would occur just when I was feeling most resentful of a people whose constant presence could in itself constitute a source of pressure, and always such gestures left me feeling dreadful that I could ever have thought ill of those capable of them.

It was not without a degree of apprehension that I parted from my husband in Madras to continue alone to Saccidananda Ashram which lies a few miles west of Tiruchirappalli in Tamil Nadu on the banks of the sacred river Cauvery, 'the Ganges of South India'. Conscious of not having got to grips with the complexity and the diversity, of not even having begun to scratch the surface of the country through which I had been travelling, that so much here was screened, subliminal, vaguely I sensed that if the many apparently divergent impressions refused to be reconciled it had something to do with the manner in which they were approached. I was certain only that what was needed was an intuitive heart, the power of a spiritual gaze. Of the man I was journeying to meet at Saccidananda Ashram I knew little but that he was an Englishman, a scholar of theology and of comparative religion, that he was a devout Christian who wore the saffron *kavi* habit of the Hindu *sannyasi*, an ascetic who was yet that rare person integrated in body, mind, heart and spirit. Such a man had chosen for more than thirty years to make India his home.

The last phase of the journey to the ashram was the occasion of another of those minor miracles to which the atmosphere of India seemed somehow more conducive. The bus on which I was due to travel to Madras airport failed to stop at the hotel and so I found myself sharing a taxi with another departing guest, a Swiss businessman who, it emerged in the course of conversation, was not only travelling to Tiruchirappalli on the same flight but also, by some extraordinary coincidence, ultimately planning to spend Easter at that remote spot on the banks of the Cauvery, Saccidananda Ashram. The drive from Tiruchirappalli was made at sunset and we spoke little as we hurtled in character-istic taxi fashion along a road which ran for a number of miles parallel to a broad canal where buffalo wallowed un-disturbed. Yet I was grateful for the silent presence of my companion as he sat cross-legged on the back seat to ease the pain of an injured back.

It was pitch dark by the time we reached the assortment of low thatched buildings that nestled amongst the palmyra trees beyond an archway inscribed with the words 'Sacci-dananda Ashram'. A Maundy Thursday Mass was in progress and the sound of *tabalas* and *tamburas* accompanying Indian *bhajans* filled the humid night air. In the temple a tall but slightly stooping figure with shoulder-length white hair and a flowing beard was administering the sacraments. He had an ascetic face with high cheek-bones and deep-set grey-blue eyes. His thin but muscular frame reflected years of hard toil under the Indian sun but, when he spoke, his voice was incongruously unadulterated 'public school'. His congregation was made up of a substantial number of Indians and Westerners. Over Easter the number of visitors swelled considerably until the small and simple thatched guest-rooms, cells to be more exact, could contain no more and people made their beds contentedly on the verandas outside.

The day at the ashram began, as days all over India begin, at dawn. The sun rising over the River Cauvery would find individuals and small groups meditating on its banks. Breakfast was preceded by community worship in the temple. The vegetarian meals were eaten Indian style, without utensils, on the floor of an unfurnished dining hall, and though ample they were simple to the point of austerity. Five times a day the community gathered in the temple to meditate and chant Hindu, Buddhist and Christian prayers. The Mass of the Indian rite which was used in the ashram reflected the cosmic symbolism of Hinduism. At the offertory water was sprinkled around the gifts and the altar, then upon the people. The celebrant himself took a sip to purify himself within. In the bread and wine, the fruits of the earth and the work of human hands were offered to the Divine. Next eight flowers were placed around the gifts in the eight directions of space to signify that the sacrifice offered was at the centre of the universe. Then incense was waved over the gifts as was fire, the flame of burning camphor. The fourfold offering of the elements was used to signify that the Mass was a cosmic sacrifice. Christ had assumed the whole creation and was offering it in and through himself to the Father. It was also a reflection of the fact that in India everything is acknowledged to have a sacred character.

In the temple here, as in Hindu temples throughout India,

worshippers could mark their foreheads with coloured powders steeped in symbolism. In the morning paste of sandalwood, a very precious wood which spreads its fragrance to others even when cut with an axe, was used to signify the grace of God; at midday a red powder, *kumkum*, was used to mark a third eye upon the forehead, the eye of internal knowledge and intuitive experience of God; in the evening *vibhudi*, ashes, served as a reminder of human mortality and of the purified self for in ashes all impurities had been burnt away. The design and symbolism of the building itself belonged to another world of symbols strange and bewildering at first to the western visitor. A wide gulf apparently separated that world from the world that featured in the conversation of the visitors who gathered in the central courtyard to talk over mid-morning coffee and afternoon tea of their affluent homes, their cars and their security. Yet there were those who bridged the gulf with no evident difficulty, and at the centre of this mystifyingly integrated life was the tall Englishman in the saffron robes of renunciation, who had made his a life of freedom from endless artificial needs. About him there was a palpable sense of unhurriedness, easy humour and calm. Life in the ashram was peaceful and slow-paced. Tuning myself to the mood, I did not press for interviews but watched and waited.

At night I lay on the hard ledge in my room, fascinated by the dance of the fire-flies and listening to the scamper of rodents in the thatching overhead and the sound of frogs croaking in the small pool outside. It was too hot to close the wooden shutters, no matter what might enter through the open window. Before crawling beneath the mosquito net I would sluice myself with buckets of cold water but within minutes the relief they brought was dispelled. Sleep was haphazard, but there it did not seem to matter. Rural India has a way of simplifying needs. By day I walked through mango groves, beneath broad-leafed banana trees or along the dusty road that led to the nearest small town of Kulitalai. The people there had a life that was beautiful in its simplicity, or so at least it seemed to a stranger from a world which delighted in continually increasing human needs and so perpetuating the dependency on material things. Three times a day I joined in the worship in the temple and often there were local people present. They differed from so many of the western visitors not simply in the colour of their skin or the style of their clothes but in ways that were far more profound. The grace of their movement, their natural beauty and warmth seemed to well spontaneously from within. Intuitively they seemed to grasp the spirit of the words inscribed upon the ground outside the temple, words which were written in English and which few of them could therefore have read. 'Every temple built outside', ran the inscription, 'is the blueprint of the destiny everyone has to reach within.'

Shantivanam –
'The Abode of Peace'

To the region washed by the River Cauvery and to that same small town of Kulitalai had come some forty years previously a French priest by the name of Jules Monchanin. Born in France on 10 April 1895, Monchanin had from the time of his adolescence felt himself drawn to India, its people, history and religion, but it was not until 1938 that he received permission from his bishop to enter the missionary community of the Société des Auxilaires des Missions and it was only in the following Spring that, after many years of patient waiting, he set out from Marseilles for the land of his vocation. At first resident in the bishop's house, in the diocese of Trichonopoly (now Tiruchirappalli), he began at once the study of Tamil and by the end of that year had been appointed curate to the village of Panneipatti. This was the beginning of a parish ministry primarily among widely scattered and often isolated Christian families in south Indian village communities, among them that of Kulitalai, of which he would become pastor for three separate periods during the years that followed. For Monchanin those years were not devoid of loneliness or physical hardship. In many ways his exceptional capacity for assimilation and his knowledge of Indian philosophy would more obviously have destined him for fruitful dialogue with Hindu spiritual leaders and a ministry among the élite of India; but a decade spent in service of the simple but, as he would discover, very warm and sensitive people of the villages would allow him to integrate his extensive knowledge of Indian thought gleaned through books with the reality of the daily life of the very poor. They were years that would enable him to develop his pastoral gifts to the full. They were also years of preparation for a contemplative life and a venture which Monchanin hoped would be a first step towards bridging the gap between the Christian culture as it existed in India at the time and the Indian culture proper.

It was in 1947 that Jules Monchanin first received a letter from Henri Le Saux, another French priest and a Benedictine monk from Saint Anne de Kergonan Abbey in Brittany. Like Monchanin, he had long recognized the spiritual riches of India. His particular calling, he had for some time felt, was to go to India and there introduce a monastic life which would be both Indian and Benedictine. The idea was one which found instant recognition in Jules Monchanin who had even before his departure for India written to a friend: 'Pray to the Holy Spirit that I will one day be a monk in a monastery born from the thought, heart, and contemplation of India and dedicated to the Holy Trinity. That is my constant thought and my one essential wish.' The approval of Le Saux' desire to come to India eventually came from Bishop Mendonca, the same bishop of Trichonopoly who had welcomed Monchanin into his diocese, and on the 15 August 1948 Father Le Saux disembarked at Colombo. After a brief stay in Trichonopoly he moved into the rectory occupied by Father Monchanin in Kulitalai and there the two men prepared for their life together with prayer, study and the exchange of ideas. What evolved from these preparations was the basis for a monastic life which, while firmly grounded in the principles and traditions of Christian monasticism, would at the same time manifest itself as the natural product of the Indian climate and yearning. Both men were convinced of the absolute necessity of a Christian contemplative life in India. Understandably, given the destitution and misery of some of India's rural poor and the great masses of people crowded into urban areas, two centuries of evangelization which had been focused on *pariahs* and the lower castes had created an overwhelming emphasis on works of mercy. The suffering and the starving were all too naturally more receptive to supernatural realities manifested in charity directed towards their basic needs. In catering to those needs, however, the two French Fathers felt, the Church in India had perhaps failed adequately to make understood the divine source of that spirit of charity. It had failed to accord to divine contemplation and Christian spirituality its proper value, and perhaps, they suggested, it was this very failure that was in some way responsible for the fact that those Indians who had become Christians were mostly people 'whom mystic and enlightened India had hardly reached'. Converts to Christianity were drawn predominantly from India's poor and uneducated. At the same time India had a profound message of spirituality of its own. Christianity, if it was to appear relevant and meaningful to the Indian people must not fail to correlate what was good in Indian wisdom and traditions with the Christian message. Nor must acceptance of Christianity appear to be identified with the acceptance of western culture. The Church must give an Indian outlook and shape to Christian life.

The message was not entirely new. The aim of the first Christian missionaries to India, of men such as De Nobili, had been to translate into action the direction of St Paul, of becoming all things to all people that they might by all means save some. They had not wanted to make Catholicism appear merely a Jewish, or Greek, or Roman religion, but had endeavoured instead to emphasize the transcendental supernatural character of Christianity untrammelled by foreign elements, and to stress its adaptability to different nations, races and cultures. De Nobili had deliberately avoided an absolute enforcement of doctrine and adopted an attitude of 'give and take' with regard to the purely social customs of India. He and others like him had, in fact, tried to make the Christian Church as much Indian as it should legitimately be, as much Indian as it was Greek or Roman or any other nationality. By living as a *sannyasi* and making a deep study of Hindu scriptures he had furthermore been able to win even Brahmins to his faith. Yet later missionaries, although in no way less committed or self-sacrificing, had not continued to work along the same lines. Even at the time when Jules

Monchanin and Henri Le Saux were pioneering their attempt to start a purely contemplative institute which, with its roots firmly planted in Christian principles of monasticism would try to bring out the best in the Indian ascetic mode of life, a time when the spirit of 'Church-Indianization' was making itself felt throughout India, Christianity was still looked upon as an imported religion and a vestige of days of alien domination.

The French Fathers held the view that it was in her monks that India's message of spirituality found its best expression. It was her monks who fully experienced what was latent in her soul, and so well had India recognized this fact that, according to her best traditions, every man after fulfilling his duties towards God and society as a 'householder', was invited to leave everything and dedicate himself, as *sannyasin*, in complete renunciation of himself and of the world, to the 'quest of Brahman, the One without a second'. Man was even to be born again and again until eventually there came the day when, by virtue of his previous good deeds and also of the gift of God, he would perceive the utter vanity of the world and pass through the supreme stage (*ashrama*) of *sannyasa*.

In attempting to delineate the essentials of their proposed Indian contemplative institute Monchanin and Le Saux were of the opinion that, initially at least, Indian monasticism must be firmly established on a well-tested Rule. The basic Rule would therefore be the so-called 'Rule of Monks' written by Saint Benedict, fourteen centuries previously. At the same time, however, they acknowledged that in contemporary Benedictine monasteries elsewhere there were many customs and practices which had no essential bearing on monastic life and which were very largely the product of a particular environment. Conventions which were social and external and alien to the Indian way of life need surely not be slavishly adhered to. In Europe, many people greeted one another by shaking hands; in India similar courtesy was shown by joining hands, *anjali*. In Europe, out of respect they un-covered their heads; in India, out of respect they removed their footwear and even uncovered their shoulders. In

Europe, people prayed kneeling; in India they liked to pray sitting cross-legged or in a prostrate position. By the observance of Indian customs of this kind Indians could be made to feel more easily at one with the Christian monastic life. Furthermore, certain elements in India's own monastic traditions could be taken into account in so far as they were as the French Fathers would write in *An Indian Benedictine Ashram*, 'in conformity with the evangelical spirit' and capable of being harmonized with Christian monastic traditions. Indian traditions – except to some degree in sects such as Buddhism or Jainism – did not possess anything comparable to the studied organization and regulations of Western Christian monasticism. Nevertheless, handed down through the ages from guru to disciple and found embodied in some of the *Shastras* and the *Upanishads* there were certain usages and traditions relating to ashrams, places where groups of disciples gathered round a guru to share in his prayer life and his experience of God, to *vanaprastha* (forest hermits) and *sannyasa*, and concerned mainly with solitude, seclusion and silence, poverty, abstinence and fasting, dress, *brahmacarya* (chastity), obedience to the guru, and meditation. Many of these elements could be quite spontaneously harmonized with the rule of St Benedict.

In India, the ancient *sannyasa* tradition placed particular emphasis on solitary life. In the first chapter of his Rule, Saint Benedict extolled the greatness of the life of the anchorite, but he was also aware that nobody could undertake such a life without a special gift from God and so he wrote his Rule for the ordinary cenobitical monks. The ashram which Monchanin and Le Saux specifically envisaged would be, like every Benedictine monastery, a community living as a family, but it was recognized that in India it might be possible to satisfy a little more the longing for solitude so congenial to Indian asceticism by building the monks' separate cells at some distance from one another. With regard to the importance of silence, there was no real conflict between the two traditions. More particularly, from sunset to sunrise, it was decided, the silence of the ashram was in no way to be disturbed.

With regard to poverty, St Benedict was anxious to remove from his disciples the 'evil of property'. In India Monchanin and Le Saux were conscious that the need for actual poverty would be even greater. The *sannyasi*'s condition was one of absolute want or dependence. In giving up his social and ritualistic duties as a 'householder' or *grihastha* he also gave up his right to possess a house of his own, to keep his own fire, to provide for his daily needs by the labour of his hands. He possessed nothing but his scanty cloth, his stick and his alms-bowl, and depended entirely on the good will of the people he encountered. When his needs were met he gave thanks to God; when he had to go without he did not complain but submitted with joy to the will of God. The surrender of the *sannyasi* to Divine Providence was the most complete that Monchanin and Le Saux could conceive. It was an ideal constantly to be borne in mind. In addition to this, the low standard of living of the country as a whole would provide a further incentive to adopting the simplest ways of life, for it could never be acceptable for monks to have a higher standard of living than their neighbours. Monks' cells would therefore be built out of the cheapest possible materials and in the manner of the most ordinary local houses. Furniture must be conformable with Indian poverty. Beds, tables and chairs would thus not normally be permitted.

As far as food was concerned, the Benedictine Rule prohibited the eating of meat and placed careful restrictions on the number of meals. Similarly, Indian *Shastras* permitted only vegetarian food. The *sannyasi*, dependent entirely on the generosity of others, was furthermore forbidden to beg his daily food before kitchen fires had been put out and 'householders' had finished their own meal. Indian Christian monastic life, as the French Fathers envisaged it, would prohibit the consumption of non-vegetarian food and of alcohol. With this restriction, in choice and preparation the monks' food would be that of the country's ordinary people.

Meals would be taken squatting on the floor, preferably served on leaves and in silence. Indian manners would be carefully observed. The dress too of the monks would be essentially that of Hindu *sannyasis*. Indian ascetics were distinguishable by their traditional *kavi*, or saffron-coloured robe, saffron because it was the colour of the sun reflected upon the earth and hence the symbol of enlightenment. Through his *kavi*, the *sannyasi* was ever recognized and treated as a man consecrated to God, devoid of any interest in the material things and the pleasures of this world. In Tamil Nadu the dress took the form of two long pieces of cotton cloth worn one round the waist and the other over the shoulders. Monks could wear wooden sandals or walk barefooted, and to distinguish them from Hindu *sannyasis* they would wear the wooden cross of St Benedict on a rosary round their necks.

'Prayer must not be considered by monks as a special occupation limited to stated intervals', Fathers Monchanin and Le Saux would write in *An Indian Benedictine Ashram*. 'Prayer should be the permanent state of their soul and the very breath of their holy life.' The prayer and the whole spiritual life of a true Benedictine monk was traditionally moulded in liturgy and Monchanin and Le Saux hoped very much that one day the liturgical Benedictine ideal would shine out in India, that the Divine Praise would one day 'be chanted in the name of the people, framed in words and set in music emanating from its soul'. For the time being, however, they suggested only that at the chief 'hours' of the day, consecrated by both Christian and Hindu traditions (that is, at sunrise, at noon and at sunset), the monks would gather in the oratory for a conventual prayer in the local language.

St Benedict had not thought it necessary to give any detailed direction about private prayer, but Fathers Monchanin and Le Saux were certain that it would be by no means inconsistent with the spirit of the Rule and at the same time quite in accordance with Indian aspirations to set apart at least one or two hours daily to 'exclusive mental prayer'. The time and duration would depend on personal inclination, the guidance of obedience and the necessary integration in common life. Such prayer could be undertaken in the oratory, the cell or even in the wood or on the riverbank.

Part of the concluding message of *An Indian Benedictine Ashram* was that in their prayers monks must remember that the true Indian *sannyasi* was one who had some intuition into the divine Transcendence and who devoted his life to its pursuit. The normal attitude of the *sannyasi*'s soul was 'an unswerving attention to God, the Absolute one'. This was symbolized in the mysterious sound OM or AUM, one sound made up of three elements, the object of his constant meditation. The true *sannyasi*, following in the footsteps of the Vedic seers and Upanishadic seekers – in order to obtain salvation from the bondage of illusion focused his mind upon the *nirguna* Brahman, the Absolute, as devoid of attributes, in its pure simplicity. For the enlightened *sannyasin*, however, conscious as he was that the Deity *has* not, but *is*, by essence, Existence, Intelligence and Beatitude, the ultimate simplicity of the Absolute could rightly be named SAT (being) CIT (knowledge) ANANDA (bliss). The Christian repeating that sacred formula SACCIDANANDA could give it a new and mysterious meaning:

> More fervently and with greater appreciation than any of his fellow-*sannyasis*, can the Christian monk utter: SAT, when thinking of the Father, the 'Principleless' Principle, the very source and end of the expansion and 'recollection' of the divine Life; CIT, when remembering the eternal Son, the Logos, the intellectual consubstantial Image of the Existent; ANANDA when meditating on the Paraclete, unifying together the Father and the Son.

These ideas were formally committed to paper in 1951, but already at the beginning of the previous year Fathers Monchanin and Le Saux had moved out of their rectory to attempt actually to live an Indian Christian monastic life. Monchanin had always been particularly attached to the countryside round Kulitalai, to the groves of coconut palms and the green rice fields, to the vast bed of the River Cauvery that flowed nearby and to the lofty blue mountains beyond. Often in the evenings when the heat of the day was over and a vermilion sun coloured everything with soft hues he had taken refuge beneath the trees on the river bank to pray and meditate. It was in an isolated spot in the very heart of a mango grove beside the Cauvery that the two French priests first constructed two flimsy shacks made out of bamboo and palm leaves. This first site was not far from that of the present ashram but it was a place where the undergrowth was more dense and conditions were particularly trying. For some months Jules Monchanin who would take the name of Swami Parama Arubi Anandam (the Bliss of the Supreme Spirit) and Henri Le Saux who was to become Swami Abhishiktananda (the Bliss of Christ) struggled to lead a contemplative existence in a place infested with snakes and scorpions and where the cries of monkeys in the night disturbed their sleep and their meditation. A succession of murders had been committed in the surrounding forest. Their health and their safety were constantly under threat and eventually they were advised to move to the less hostile location of the present ashram at Shantivanam, the 'abode of peace'.

On the feast of St Benedict 1950 the official foundation of the ashram, a monastery in Indian style focusing on a trinitarian spirituality, was marked by a solemn Mass, and on 11 October of the same year an oratory built in the style of a Hindu temple, without decoration to convey the idea of the emptying of the soul before the Absolute, and with an altar and a tabernacle of solid unpolished granite, was blessed. This temple in which the sanctuary took the form of a *mulasthanam* and to which a narthex for the people was attached in the style of a *mandapam*, was located at the entrance to the hermitage to emphasize its availability to people from the nearby village. What Saccidananda Ashram's founders envisaged was the first nucleus of a monastery, something in the nature of a *laura*, a grouping of neighbouring anchorites like the ancient *laura* of Saint Sabas in Palestine. Jules Monchanin's desire was that 'what is deepest in Christianity may be grafted on to what is deepest in India'. 'Our *Advaita* (non-duality) and the praise of the Trinity are our only aim', he wrote and in so doing put his finger on what would in time come to be recognized as the precise point at which the meeting in depth between Indian spirituality and the Christian faith must take place.

Sadly, it was Father Monchanin's vocation not to reach the goal to which he aspired, but to open the way for others. In his lifetime he would see the construction of three huts, a small library, refectory and a guest house, but at no time did the number of ashramites exceed six. Currents of suspicion and misunderstanding arose in connection with the two foreign priests who wore *kavi* and sought to transubstantiate and crystallize the search of the Hindu *sannyasi*. Indian Catholics had for too long been told that Hinduism was a diabolic invention for them not to be surprised and disconcerted by an understanding and sympathetic attitude. At the most obvious level of the integration of Indian rather than western social customs into the Christian life the French Fathers' ideas were difficult enough for the local community to accept. Their more profound message, that what was necessary was for Christians and Hindus to go to the *source* of their respective religions before they had developed into systems and theologies, and that at that source a true meeting could take place, was simply beyond the theological and philosophical capabilities of many. *An Indian Benedictine Ashram* was written in an attempt to justify theologically the two priests' position both in the Church and in India. Bishop Mendonca endorsed that position with a foreword stressing that the two energetic recluses living in a remote corner of his diocese had his full approval for their novel way of life and were prepared to abide by the direction of any legitimate authority. Nonetheless the hoped-for vocations were not forthcoming. Monchanin and Le Saux were many years ahead of their time.

Perhaps it should also be said that the austere life of the two priests did little to encourage even those friends, priests or religious, who were sympathetic to their ideas. The strictly

vegetarian Indian food, the absence of furniture apart from
cots and a few shelves to prevent the termites from eating
their books, the fact that the only bath took the form of the
Cauvery River, and the threat of floods which at times meant
that the ashram had to be evacuated did little to attract those
not drawn to extreme asceticism. Criticized on one occasion
because the ashram was too 'miserable', Monchanin's
response was that the Hindu *sannyasi* went much further in
the emptying of self. More humorously he added that he
would gladly consent to owning a bath when every Indian
family was equipped with one. In part, at least, it was the
self-imposed rigours of his ascetic life that would eventually
cause the death of this deeply spiritual man. He had always
wanted to die in his beloved India but even that aspiration was
to be denied him. Instead, at the insistence of friends, his last
days were spent in a hospital in Paris where he died on 10
October 1957 as a result of a tumour located near the stomach
and of a number of other minor ailments.

In human terms Monchanin's mission appeared to have
been a failure. Nor did the ashram show much sign of
increased growth in the period immediately following his
death. If anything, in the absence of the man who had been
for many years loved and respected as the parish priest of
Kulitalai, relations with the local people deteriorated.
Between 1952 and 1956 Henri Le Saux had spent long periods
in caves on the side of the sacred mountain of Arunachala in
contact with Hindu hermits and disciples of the *advaitin*
sage, Sri Ramana Maharshi. After making a pilgrimage to the
sources of the Ganges in the Spring of 1959, Father Le Saux
dreamed of returning there and eventually, in 1962, set up a
small hermitage in Utterkashi not far from the sources of the
sacred river. It was there that he would write his chief works
and continue to stress that diversity did not necessarily mean
disunity, once the Centre of all had been reached. While
always adhering firmly to his faith in Christ, Abhishiktananda became equally convinced of the validity of the
'*advaitic* experience' and its expression in the life of *sannyasa*.
Yet these two spiritual experiences, which both claimed to be

ultimate, were apparently irreconcilable. He never abandoned his belief that the truth in each of them must eventually converge, but was compelled to acknowledge that any intellectual formulation of that convergence could only be reached in the distant future, if ever. In the meantime he stressed the need for an *inward* approach to all problems of diversity of religious conviction. The real meeting point was in the 'cave of the heart', in which all true experiences of the Spirit welled up as from their source.

Swami Abhishiktananda died at Indore in 1973. By that time the Second Vatican Council had brought about not merely a transformation of the externals of the Church but also a new climate in which the necessity for Christians to enter into dialogue with all men of good will was widely accepted. By that time also his vision and the vision of Jules Monchanin who had so often quoted the words of Christ, 'Unless the seed die, it cannot bear fruit abundantly' (John 12.24–5) had indeed begun to bear fruit. The influence of their thinking was spreading, and the small ashram at Shantivanam had begun to grow, under the guidance of an English Benedictine monk, Dom Bede Griffiths.

3

Journey towards God

Dom Bede Griffiths, or Alan Richard Griffiths as he was christened, was born on 17 December 1906 in his parents' home in Walton-on-Thames. He was the youngest of four children and, to use his sister's expression, 'rather his mother's Benjamin'. His ancestors on both sides were farming people but Walter Griffiths, Alan's father, had been taken into an uncle's paint business in Liverpool at an early age and worked as an analytical chemist. He was made a partner in the firm. On the uncle's death, however, he himself took a partner who in time squeezed Walter Griffiths out of the business. Alan's father remains a somewhat veiled presence in his son's autobiographical account in *The Golden String* and is still not a subject readily elaborated upon, but from the accounts of others who knew the family there emerges the impression of a man who was charming, kindly and popular but who failed to pull his weight. Certainly, he appears not to have been a driving force in the home. Acknowledging that public life might well have been an area in which Walter Griffiths could have succeeded, Father Bede refers with indulgence to the manner in which his father would talk and talk on politics. The rest of the family simply acquired the habit of letting him go on without affording him undue attention. The law suit which Walter Griffiths instigated against his former partner failed and, despite a natural generosity of spirit which prevented him from regarding the man as anything but a friend, he never really recovered from the experience. There are intimations of a 'breakdown'. Having lost all his money, in retirement Walter Griffiths passed some of his time playing golf, and not without a certain degree of success.

Consequently it was to Alan's mother, Harriet Lilian

Frampton-Day, a relative of Henry Fielding, that most of the responsibility for the running of the home and the upbringing of the children fell. It was a task undertaken not without a struggle for restricted finances must have made the maintenance of the kind of expectations associated with what Father Bede has referred to as a 'typical English middle-class family' difficult. Nevertheless, it was one to which she rose in a way which was impressive. Because of the reduction in their fortunes, while Alan was still too young fully to appreciate the reason for the change, the family moved from Walton-on-Thames to the village of New Milton on the edge of the New Forest. At that time there could be no question of Harriet Griffiths, or Lilian as she was always known, going out to work but she did virtually all the work in the house in New Milton herself, something for which her own upbringing could hardly have prepared her, and held the family together on her own small private income in such a way that the children were not conscious of any particular deprivation. They learned at an early age how to do domestic chores, how to clean and to help with the cooking, but for this experience of work and 'comparative poverty' Father Bede has since been grateful, and it appears only to have been some of the luxuries that went missing from their lives.

Like his brothers, Alan was sent to Furzie Close preparatory school at Barton-on-Sea, not far from New Milton. Dudley was four years older and Laurence three years older than Alan. Barbara, the only daughter, came between Laurence and the youngest child. In later life Dudley would join the merchant navy and afterwards become a travelling rep. for a jewellery firm, Laurence taught at various schools and eventually became headmaster of Salisbury Cathedral School and Barbara would become a school matron, but it was Alan who was always regarded as the brains of the family. Recognizing his ability, his mother had had him taught French at the age of four in a small kindergarten school. By the time he was seven and at Furzie Close he was well versed in Latin and generally excelled academically. Furzie Close was a private school run by a married couple and frequented by its fair share of the children of the nobility. It was here that Alan became quite friendly with Frank Pakenham, the future Lord Longford, whom he would encounter again at Oxford. Alan experienced no real difficulties at his preparatory school. Looking back on it he sees in the way it was run 'a typical sort of tyranny'. Those who were unfortunate enough to cross either the man or his wife who ran it were slapped on the face. In this and similar treatment Father Bede discerns a certain cruelty, a lesser but similar strain of cruelty to that which caused his friend of later years, C.S. Lewis, such distress at his Hertfordshire prep school; but then Lewis' first headmaster was eventually committed to a lunatic asylum and Lewis was later so unhappy at his public school, Malvern (which he referred to as 'Wyvern'), that he was taken away to be educated by a private tutor. Alan Griffiths on the other hand escaped for the most part such rough handling and achieved a rather effortless success thanks to teaching which he acknowledges was good.

The choice of Christ's Hospital, the famous Blue-Coat school, as the place where all three sons would continue their education was Lilian Griffiths'. Founded by Edward VI for the 'relief of the poor', it had retained its original character as a charity school. Payment was made according to income and entrants were required to have presentations and to pass an entrance exam. When it came to Alan's turn to take the exam, he passed first out of over a hundred applicants, a fact which meant that he went straight into the 'broady' form, so-called because its members wore a broad girdle. A new boy in a 'broady' was a sufficiently rare sight to attract attention and a source of satisfaction to a mother who was particularly close to her youngest child. On the train, travelling to Christ's Hospital, another mother accompanying her son remarked of him that he had passed second in the entrance exam. 'My boy passed first,' was Lilian Griffiths' response. It was a demonstration of maternal pride that was to remain with her son.

For Father Bede school-days conjure up memories of

standing up in class to recite irregular Latin and Greek verbs. Boys who made a mistake lost ten marks. More serious offences meant joining the queue outside the classroom to await a beating. Fear was constantly in the background and yet it was not a serious source of worry. Even when the classics teacher who had at first favoured Alan for his interest in irregular verbs sensed the transference of the boy's affections to poetry, Alan rode his disapproval without undue difficulty. The teachers were, he felt, good men who had their pupils' interests at heart, and life was always full of other distractions. Alan was always inclined to be somewhat bookish but this did not preclude interest in other things. He was very musical. At home on Sundays the family would gather round the piano to sing Moody and Sankey hymns. Walter Griffiths was fond of playing the piano and singing, and both Laurence and Alan had inherited their father's vocal gifts. Alan sang in choirs as treble, alto and tenor. He was also a talented pianist. On one occasion he played Debussy's *Clair de Lune* in the school concert. The success of his performance is something which in later life he can assess with a detachment he is able to apply to many aspects of his experience: 'I must have played quite well, you know. Somebody said it was worth coming to the concert just to hear me play.' By his own admission it took him a long time to learn, but with time he knew an entire repertoire of Chopin, Schubert, Brahms and Bach off by heart. Music would remain a great interest in his university years when he would go to concerts whenever possible, and he looked upon the interest in music as one creative element in an otherwise very sceptical Oxford.

Despite his housemaster's reference to him as 'one of those useless Grecians' (Grecians being those who belonged to the top academic form), Alan was also reasonably good at games. Laurence excelled at running and ran for Christ's Hospital in spite of a weak heart. In an educational establishment such as theirs, being good at sport was half the battle and although, as he progressed through the school, this emphasis was one which Alan rather rejected, he had a strong physique and played in the rugby team. He was also very interested in cricket. At home in New Milton the Griffiths children played French cricket and cricket together and Barbara remembers her younger brother rushing to collect the paper to follow the results of the test match. Life on the edge of the New Forest was very much an outdoor existence. Barbara would eagerly await the return of her brothers for the school holidays to join in their walks, games and cycle rides. Their home was an average sized family house with a small garden and two gates and the children would ride round the house, in one gate and out of the other. In imagination their bicycles became motorbikes. Indeed, in the absence of cinema and other similar entertainment imagination was a powerful resource. As a small boy Alan, or 'Cupid' as Dudley nicknamed him then, had an imaginary friend who was invariably responsible for leaving the garden tap on and other such minor misdemeanours. His imaginative gift did not diminish as he grew older.

The fact that Alan's father could not really relate to his wife did not mean that in general the family was not a close and a happy one. The children saw less of their Liverpool relatives than their mother's family simply because of the distance involved, but on their mother's side was a large Victorian family compiled of doctors, lawyers and successful business men who were all devoted to each other in a somewhat reserved way. Alan's childhood was conspicuously untouched by serious disruption. The children had the usual bouts of measles and chickenpox, but they never knew what it was to witness the serious illness or death of anybody close to them. A close friend of Lilian Griffiths became mentally ill but that fact was kept carefully in the background. One cousin was actually divorced and that came as an immense shock to the family but otherwise the kind of stable order associated with the middle class of the day prevailed. In Alan's home there was plenty of affection and kindness, yet there was in that very affection what he would later perceive as 'the emotional barrenness of an English middle class family'. Even between Alan and the mother to whom he professed to be very close there was little demonstration of emotion. At school boys referred to their mothers as 'the mater', an expression which seemed to epitomize the repression which characterized such family relationships. With the wisdom of hindsight it would become evident to Father Bede that beneath the surface all cannot have been flowing quite as smoothly as it appeared to be but at the time he was barely conscious of human suffering. It was not therefore that he was lacking in such qualities as compassion. It was simply that they had not been called out.

The same, after many years in India he would make a point of intimating, was true of any sexual feelings he might have had. Sex was never mentioned in the family. His mother once told him that she had banished his father from her bedroom as soon as she had had her last child and that was it. She was not interested in sex at all and on the whole, Father Bede implies, this was also true of her children. When Alan was about sixteen his eldest brother gave him a small book entitled *What a Young Man Ought to Know*. At school sex made its presence felt in the form of sex language – 'everyone was a bastard or something like that' – but otherwise sex did not come into his conversation or his life. Consequently human beings did not really have any sex. As it happened, inevitably most of his friends were male. During the holidays he met his sister's friends and female relatives. There were tennis parties, at other people's houses because the Griffiths had no tennis court, and there were other social events at which he was happy to encounter female company, but in general the circles in which he moved were male. They were also very intellectual. One boy at school in particular became a kind of model for Alan. At sixteen he knew everything there was to know and cultivated a form of intellectual snobbery that fed upon quotations such as that benign and humane line from Horace, 'I hate the profane crowd'. He and others like him exerted a strong and not always good influence on Alan Griffiths.

Another powerful influence was introduced when W.H. Fyfe succeeded Dr Upcott as headmaster of Christ's

Hospital. He was a warm and friendly man who encouraged individuals to find their own fulfilment. The first non-clergyman to head the school, he was a great humanist and a classical scholar but a man with modern ideas who enlarged the school library and opened it up to the boys. His advent was for Alan a form of renaissance. With new encouragement, he became an extraordinarily avid reader, retreating at times to the bathroom at night to indulge in private his interest in Dickens, Milton, Shakespeare, Maupassant, Hardy, Tolstoy and a multitude of other authors, often indiscriminately chosen but nonetheless potent in their impact. Reading stimulated an already prominent intellect and an active imagination. It also shaped his view of life and of religious belief.

By his own account, Alan Griffiths received little religious instruction in his youth. Yet both of his parents had a religious faith about which they spoke little but which was nevertheless strong. On Sundays, when Alan was small the family would walk to the village church in New Milton, the children dressed in sailor suits and hats, and from the country parson he acquired a respect and affection for the Church of England which is interwoven with all his childhood memories. His recollection of his mother is often of her kneeling by her bed in prayer as she did regularly morning and night throughout her life. Not long before she died, Lilian Griffiths confided to her son an experience which she had had during the early days when she was struggling to maintain the house in New Milton. Exhausted and desperate, she had seen herself one day in a mirror surrounded by an extraordinary light, a phenomenon which Father Bede would later be able to regard as an indication of God's blessing on her life.

Consciously or unconsciously something of the religious awareness of his parents must have communicated itself to the son. At the age of eight or nine, on Sunday evenings he would conduct the entire evening service, chanting the responses and saying the prayers to himself in bed. A friend of his mother had made him learn the Beatitudes and the tenth and fourteenth chapters of St John's Gospel by heart. His understanding of what he learnt was at the time necessarily limited but he would carry those passages in his memory for years. When Alan was fourteen, the family moved to the Isle of Wight to live in Sandown in a flat at the top of a house owned by an uncle who was a doctor. It was at a little church in nearby Yaverland that he remembers first encountering a 'High Church' service and experiencing a strong attraction to it without being actually able to define whether that attraction was aesthetic or religious.

At Christ's Hospital under Dr Upcott the religion was severely Protestant. Alan attended services in the school chapel every day and twice on Sundays. For his confirmation he learnt the Catechism by heart, and he listened 'spellbound' to the sermons of William Fyfe founded upon Christian humanism and preached unconventionally from the lectern in the centre of the chapel. Thus, despite the purported lack of religious instruction, religion, whether accepted or rejected, was very much a presence in his life. In any event, at the age of fifteen he began, as he would afterwards put it, to think for himself, a process influenced by the books he was reading to such an extent that when in later life he came to write *The Golden String* he was able to see that early stage in his progression towards the Christian faith in terms of a series of logical steps each accompanied by and to a substantial extent dependent on a course of reading. From Thomas Hardy Alan gleaned an awareness of the rhythm of nature and a sense of the tragedy of existence which, despite his own lack of any real contact with suffering, spoke to an awakening realization in him, born perhaps of his study of Greek classical tragedy, that it was tragedy that revealed the deepest human values. In *Tess of the D'Urbervilles* he identified a conception of God as an impersonal uncompassionate power which derived pleasure in toying with humanity. It was a concept which found a certain recognition in one who already held *King Lear* in high regard. Giovanni Papini's *Story of Christ* gave him an affection for Christ as a man but if he revered Christ it was at that time simply as a perfect human being and much as he revered Socrates. Again, after reading *Kingdom of Heaven*, in which Tolstoy portrayed his interpretation of the Sermon on the Mount, the contents of the sermon became for Alan Griffiths a personal ideal of conduct. It was Tolstoy's ideal of non-resistance to evil which most impressed him. Refusal to take rank as a lance-corporal in the Officers' Training Corps became a means by which he could express his own pacifist views, views which were not very popular in the school at large but which Mr Fyfe handled with tolerance and tact. Alan and three friends who shared his reluctance to be members of the Corps were eventually released from it altogether.

Inspired in part by Shaw, in part by Ramsay Macdonald, and doubtless also by Mr Fyfe who was a socialist, during the period of the first Labour Government of 1924, Alan too became a socialist. Together with the plays of Ibsen and Galsworthy, the works of George Bernard Shaw became to him a standard of criticism of the prevailing social order. No doubt there was in Alan's rebellion a strong element of the new generation rejecting the values of the old, but even some years later he would still see it as part of a much wider revolt unleashed by the war. Shaw was also to reinforce in Alan Griffiths a certain scepticism towards Christianity which his reading in general had led him to believe was a thing of the past. The religion in which he had been raised now seemed to him devoid of relevance and meaning. Like so many others amongst his contemporaries, and indeed like William Fyfe, the young man could not accept the importance of dogma. He rejected the belief in any authority beyond reason and the idea of any absolute moral law beyond a kind of tacitly acknowledged code of acceptable behaviour. At the time that code prohibited, together with stealing, cheating and similar offences, the display of affection and emotions and so poetry became for Alan Griffiths a form of emotional outlet. He read Wordsworth, Shelley, Keats and Blake, and through them he came to a kind of worship of nature and to an appreciation of God as the inscrutable mystery behind it.

School-days were for Alan Griffiths overwhelmingly intellectual but 'frightfully happy'. He was one of those gifted classical scholars who had a struggle to pass maths for his School Certificate but this does not seem seriously to have impaired his enjoyment. Under a liberal headmaster with a talent for 'picking out the boy of character and giving him all he'd got' Alan flourished. He had the gifts of leadership necessary to qualify him to become captain of his house during his final year and applied to Oxford almost as a matter of course as the place to which one normally went to read classics. New College was his first choice but he failed to gain a place there. Walking round Oxford, however, he fell for the architectural beauty of Magdalen and decided that this was the college for him. He reapplied and this time was awarded an Exhibition for fifty pounds a year. His position during his last terms at school allowed him greater personal freedom. He was given permission to give up sport and instead indulged his love of nature on long walks and cycle rides in the Sussex countryside. At home also he was able to nurture this love which was very deep and which had something of a religious quality about it. The family home was by this time a small house on a common near Newbury and there too he was able to seek solitude and silence and to experience a sense of the mysterious presence reflected in all that nature had to offer.

It was one evening during his last term at school that he experienced an occurrence which he would later regard as one of the decisive events in his life. As he was walking alone the sound of birdsong at sunset came to him as he had never heard it before. A hawthorn tree, the sun setting over the playing fields, a lark singing on the wing and the veil of dusk which covered the earth appeared to him then with an intensity and a beauty that filled him with overwhelming awe. It was an experience of mystical exaltation in the presence of nature that was in a sense beyond all verbal expression but it was one which Father Bede would outline years later to great effect in *The Golden String*. The title of the book was drawn from William Blake's poem:

I give you the end of a golden string:
Only wind it into a ball,
It will lead you in at heaven's gate,
Built in Jerusalem's Wall.

Father Bede's account of his evening walk alone bore witness to the way in which an experience which breaks through the routine of ordinary life could be the bearer of a message to the soul. He had walked those playing fields before but never before had he seen them in quite the same light. That evening his consciousness had been awakened to another dimension of existence. For a moment he had glimpsed his life in its true perspective in relation to eternity and suddenly he knew that he belonged to another world. Years later he would write of his conviction that his experience was by no means unique. Many experienced such moments but often their significance was lost. To him his vision was an intimation of the grace given to every soul, hidden under the circumstances of daily life and easily lost if not attended to. It was the end of Blake's 'golden string'. 'To follow up the vision which we have seen, to keep it in mind when we are thrown back again on the world, to live in its light and to shape our lives by its law, is to wind the string into a ball, and to find our way out of the labyrinth of life.' His experience was not one which would lead him straight to the nearest church, but it was one not unrelated to what he would later call 'the sense of the sacred' and one which would enable him to look upon his life in this world as a journey towards God.

4

Oxford

When Alan Griffiths went up to Oxford in October 1925, Magdalen was very much the college for old Etonians and for the kind of old Etonians who enjoyed the activities of the wealthy set to the full. Trinity, Cambridge or New College were the primary choices of Eton's more dedicated and conscientious students. Magdalen at that time received the more sociably inclined. In the recollection of one of Father Bede's contemporaries theirs was a particularly bad year. After two years in college he remembers being able to claim that not a single night had passed without somebody breaking something up. The vogue was to get drunk and go on the rampage, cracking whips and blowing hunting horns, to which the college authorities did not take undue exception provided such scourges were kept within the confines of the college grounds. Offset against those who indulged in activities of this kind were the scholars who were obliged to live cheaply and work hard. It would be strange perhaps if experience of such a gulf had not served to heighten the awareness of social injustice in one whose mother had to struggle to supplement his Exhibition.

At Oxford, initially at least, Alan became more staunchly socialist although there is nothing to suggest that this was as a result of dissatisfaction with his own personal circumstances. Socialism and pacifism were flourishing movements in Oxford then and Alan, along with numerous others, among them Michael Stewart whom he had known since school-days and who would hold political office under Harold Wilson, joined the Labour Club. It was at about that time that he

48

remembers embarrassing his mother acutely by refusing to wear formal evening dress to an evening engagement, insisting instead upon accompanying her in an ordinary dark suit. The General Strike took place in 1926. Alan supported the miners, but by his own admission, it is doubtful whether he recognized the full implications of the General Strike and the extent of his active political involvement seems to have been restricted to offering to sell copies of the *Daily Worker*. He had begun to feel very deeply the injustice of social differences but his insights were still very largely gleaned from books.

Yet another division prevailed amongst Alan Griffiths' fellow undergraduates, namely that between 'athletes' and 'aesthetes'. The main body of his contemporaries were athletes; the aesthetes formed a smaller but nonetheless influential group who took as their model the archetypal aesthete, the homosexual Oscar Wilde. Alan adored Wilde as a writer. He was fascinated too by Walter Pater and indeed by the whole of the aesthetic movement of which they formed a part. Even whilst still at school he had dubbed 1880 his model year. He himself had yearned from the age of seventeen or eighteen to become a creative writer. Literature was always an absorbing passion and the world of the visual arts also had been opened up to him at an early age during his forays through Christ's Hospital library. He had discovered a book entitled *Six Centuries of Painting*, one which as an adult he would doubtless have found limited, but one which contained illustrations of the works of all the great painters from Giotto onwards. The enthusiasm for art kindled in his boyhood would lead him thereafter to spend hours in the National Gallery and the British Museum. He became a particular admirer of Stanley Spencer. He also collected. With the help of an expert at the British Museum he became the owner of some beautiful Japanese prints which he hung in his rooms at Oxford. He also acquired two mezzotints by Whistler.

It is not difficult to establish for which social group Alan Griffiths' intellectual and artistic tastes would qualify him. As to the sexual predilections of Oscar Wilde's followers, they were by this time something of which he was not unaware. He remained, however, more interested in literature and art. During one of his vacations, his eldest brother Dudley took him on a tour of Montmartre with the object of furthering his sexual education. The world of the Paris nightclubs came as no particular shock to Alan. To him it was the world of Maupassant which he knew well from his reading and even from his own writing for at school he had so admired the French writer that he had composed, not without some success, short stories in the style of Maupassant. He had read too Flaubert's *Madame Bovary*, Stendhal's *Le Rouge et le Noir* and numerous other French novels, and although he felt the tour of Montmartre to be good for him in a sense he applied to the world of real sex the same 'look on' attitude that he did to the world of love and sex in literature. Alan was taken by Dudley round the cabarets (excluding, he would later suspect, some of the most shocking) together with a friend who lived with a prostitute. The prostitute he found to be 'an awfully nice woman' who confided to him that her one ambition in life was to get married and have a family. With the lack of inhibition born of many years in India he could now append the comment: 'Though she was very good, I believe, and Michael enjoyed it with her.'

It was the reading of D.H. Lawrence that brought Alan to the recognition that by living so exclusively on his conscious mind he might have been repressing the unconscious life of instinct. He was introduced to the works of Lawrence by Hugh l'Anson Fausset, a very dynamic young man who lived very close to the Griffiths' cottage in Newbury and whom Alan first met at a tennis party. Hugh was the son of a Northern Ireland clergyman against whom he reacted very strongly. He was also a literary critic for the *Times Literary Supplement* and steeped in modern literature. Hugh was some years older than Alan and exercised a tremendous influence on him. His introduction of Alan to such works as *Fantasia of the Unconscious* led the younger man to a new appreciation of the unconscious soul with its deep instinctive feelings and its power of intuition. Lawrence also awakened in him the recognition of the power of sex as an instinct that could only be suppressed at peril. Oxford following the

Great War was stamped with a prevailing permissiveness and there was a time at Oxford when as a general principle Alan Griffiths felt that sexual feelings should be freely expressed, but it was only for a relatively short period and it was never a principle to which he felt personally deeply attracted. His quarrel with morality, which was a contributory factor in his rejection of orthodox Christianity, was based on the idea that law and morality were evil in so far as they were separated from love, much as the rational mind was a source of ugliness when divorced from imagination. It was a quarrel that belonged very much in the realm of ideas. His friendships with men and women remained largely intellectual and it was in his love of the beauty of nature and his feeling for poetry that he identified at least a partial release for the suppressed unconscious side of his being.

Lawrence had led Alan Griffiths to see sex as an instinct that was essentially 'sacred'. The evil of immorality was thus not simply that of self-indulgence but, as he would write in *The Golden String,* 'the profanation of something sacred, the desecration of a holy instinct which arises out of the depths of our unconscious being and is the bearer of life or death'. It was an idea which Alan Griffiths extended to embrace the evil of the civilization in which he found himself. Primitive man might well be immoral, brutal and superstitious but he retained a sense of the 'sacred'. He maintained contact with the 'inner sources of life' and for that reason his existence was imbued with both dignity and beauty. The modern western world with all its science, its reason and its morality had lost this sense of the sacred and it was for this reason that its minds were sterile and its works were devoid of beauty.

The view that it was the growing gulf between science and the rational mind and the power of instinct, feeling and imagination that was the root of all the evil in the post-First World War world and that the ugliness of contemporary architecture, for example, was attributable to the fact that the mind that created it was no longer in harmony with nature, was one which was shared by two close friends who began to occupy a prominent place in Alan Griffiths' life at Magdalen.

Father Bede's recollection of his first encounter with one of them, Hugh Waterman, is of a totally unexpected conversation one night at dinner in hall when Hugh turned to him without preface and enquired whether he liked the letters of Keats. In fact, Hugh Waterman had the previous night sat across the tables from him and seen him, his eyes alight in his dark face and with a characteristic quick gesture of his right hand, expounding, and he had felt almost certain of a kindred spirit. As it happened, it was an inspired intuition, for they found at once that they shared many ideas about nature and about poetry.

Hugh was a demonstrative, affectionate man with a great gift for friendship. He had been unhappy at Marlborough, despite the fact that he was able to recognize that it had given him many good things, among them close contact with the Downs, the capacity to win some prizes and the ability to play the organ. What he regarded as an unfortunate misunderstanding had placed him in the top athletic house in which severe penalties were meted out for ineptitude at games. Hugh could never throw a cricket ball straight although in later life he would remark with pride that he could throw a bull to trim his feet or back a horse with a loaded waggon through a barn door. As a schoolboy he took refuge in the poetry and prose he read and made of them and of his happier home his real life. At home he was open to far more feminine influence than Alan Griffiths and something of this, together with his many other gifts, he brought to their friendship. The fact that Hugh always had flowers in his room, had a copy of Botticelli's *Primavera* on the wall, and could express his concern for the socially underprivileged by emptying his pockets for a poor man, found a particular resonance in one whose experience of life was very masculine and essentially undemonstrative. Hugh Waterman looked upon the story of St Francis of Assisi, his joy in the marvel of the everyday, the humility, humanity and humour of his faith, as one of the most potent inspirations of his life, and there was about Hugh something of the spirit of the saint he admired.

'A typical English pragmatist' is how Alan once described Hugh. Nonetheless Hugh was a writer of romantic poetry. It was Martyn Skinner, Hugh's tutorial partner, however, who would become the serious poet, the winner in 1943 of the Hawthornden Prize. At school at Clifton under a master who later published a book on poetic diction, Martyn had begun to write satire in the style of the Augustan poets, directed for the most part against the athletic heroes who dominated the school. He had failed, in his own view 'stupidly', to anticipate the reaction to his satire, found himself very unpopular, and as a result appeared during the early days at Magdalen slightly embittered and aloof. Hugh was able to perceive the shyness that lay behind the veneer. Martyn had won the scholarship for which Hugh had tried. They found themselves sharing their weekly tutorial and thereafter became almost constant companions for the next few years.

Martyn had an understanding of business and politics which far outreached Hugh's or Alan's. His father, Sir Sydney Skinner, was Chairman of one of London's first department stores and had been largely responsible for generating the very form of modern commercialism that Alan and Hugh and Martyn detested. Yet Sir Sydney was also a man of mental and moral stature who instinctively commanded respect. Of him his son would write on one occasion, 'he loved his fellow men but had no illusions about them', and a remark he made to Martyn would remain with Hugh Waterman for many years. As he stood with his son watching the store's new building going up Sir Sydney Skinner commented: 'Much of what people will buy in there they don't really need, and some they would be better without.' Without wishing to imply that a man is purely the mechanism of his genes, Hugh Waterman would later suggest that with this behind him, an uncle who was a brilliant inventor and his mother's Cornish intensity, it was easier to understand how Martyn's scepticism about contemporary notions of progress grew. More readily comprehensible too was his passionate conviction that ugliness was not merely an abuse or a breach of taste but a corrosive evil which ate away at the spirit of man.

Martyn Skinner has claimed that it was Hugh, whose own sense of belonging to nature was powerfully present even during school cross-country runs – 'when you swung into your rhythm with your second wind, you felt an elemental creature, elemental like the north wind that beat and chafed you' - who first opened his eyes to Nature as Wordsworth understood Nature. Hugh Waterman's own view was that it was only a matter of time and circumstance before Martyn rediscovered the country heritage his great-grandfather had left when he walked from Devon to London: 'Strip the jacket off most Englishmen, and you have a would-be farmer at heart.' Whether or not Martyn was being too generous in his acclaim of his friend, the fact remained that they both came to the belief that what was nearest to Nature was good, a belief which they shared with Alan Griffiths who, following his experience at school and his reading of Wordsworth, had made the spirit of nature the object of his worship. Together the three of them went on long country walks, thinking nothing of walking thirty miles a day. Together they appreciated the beauty of Magdalen's historic buildings, built at a time when the creative spirit of man was in harmony with the natural world surrounding him, and together they abhorred the ugliness of modern suburbs spreading out from Cowley. By this time Alan Griffiths' socialism had changed in emphasis. It was no longer the material poverty of the industrial workers that most disturbed him but rather the fact that a much broader section of humanity was being deprived of the natural beauty to which it had a right.

For Alan himself Oxford provided the ideal setting for the life he wished to lead. For part of the time he had digs in Iffley Road and in his final year he moved further out of Oxford to an old farm-house from which he could indulge his love of country walking to the full. Initially, however, he had rooms in college in the eighteenth century 'New Buildings' over-looking the cloisters. In detail he observed the seasonal changes along the riverbanks of Oxford and made of them a backcloth for his studies. The waterways were relatively uncongested then and in the summer months he and Hugh and Martyn would take punts out on the river and remain there till nightfall reading not, significantly, Latin or Greek, but Spenser's *Faerie Queene* and Sir Philip Sidney's *Arcadia*. Two memories of Alan Griffiths in his Oxford days Hugh Waterman would record in his old age. One was an occasion when he visited Alan at home near Newbury and together they walked through the woods, trying to identify birds by sound and not by sight, to talk to Stanley Spencer who was then painting his 'Resurrection' on the East wall of the Sandham Chapel. The other was a night in Hugh's rooms when they talked of Milton in the firelight and Alan began to read *Paradise Lost* aloud to him, not ending until three o'clock in the morning. Martyn was supposed to be reading history but he too read the same books which then became the subject for debate.

In 1927 an Oxford friend of Martyn Skinner who was interested in Celtic mythology planned a visit to County Kerry to collect legends. Martyn in turn involved Hugh and Alan and the four of them set off for the west coast of Ireland. They pitched their tent in what Father Bede would later describe in *The Golden String* as 'perhaps the wildest and most primitive place which we ever found'. There were one or two cottages in the vicinity. Provisions were bought from the village of Ballyferriter some six miles away but otherwise they were free to enjoy the solitude and the scenic beauty they sought. Martyn was particularly dedicated to natural scenery and, in his own words, 'spent days just mooning around'. The instigator of the expedition spent his time collecting legends and Hugh, who was possibly the most sociable of the group, used to go out and 'talk to the natives'. Alan certainly enjoyed and appreciated the wild and undisturbed beauty of West Kerry but he was not quite as exhilarated by it as Martyn, who remembers his friend being very romantic and reading with relish but without affectation, works such as *Hamlet* which he felt appropriate to the scenery. Martyn Skinner's memories are tinged with characteristic humour but the stay on those wild rugged cliffs overlooking the Atlantic rollers remains one of the great experiences of his life, and Father Bede's description of the experience and of the Ballyferriter cliffs speaks eloquently of their impact upon him. Many years later in 1980 that description would inspire an Irish journalist to write an article about the camp, in response to which several people contacted him saying that they clearly remembered the strange group of young men of 53 years earlier but that they had not had the slightest idea 'what Alan Griffiths and his companions were about'. In retrospect Father Bede would see the stay in West Kerry as part of the unconscious search for God. At the time he would still have thought in terms of imagination, the source of creative power, which they sought to awaken in themselves by living in close communion with nature and with those works of man that had been created in harmony with nature. It was this kind of aspiration which induced them on another occasion to break into Rievaulx Abbey to view the ruins by moonlight. Having been refused entry at the front, they gained illicit access through the back to what, in the light of the full moon, was another rare experience.

In those days it was not uncommon for undergraduates not to finish their course. Neither Hugh nor Martyn remained at Oxford at that juncture to take their degree but Alan Griffiths did. He got a second but took his failure to achieve the first, for which he had hoped and for which his tutor had felt he was qualified, philosophically – 'On the whole I have always recognized that academically I am a good second class.' Alan never collected his MA. Nor was the degree which he actually took in Greats, the course on which he had originally embarked. Having passed his classical Honour Moderations with five alphas, only two short of the seven required for first class, he opted instead to read English. His choice was primarily the product of the conviction he had reached that purely intellectual knowledge was of little value and that it was through poetry and imagination and not through reason and intellect that fulfilment was to be found. It was also one which would have a significant impact on the life that followed, not least because it brought him into contact with C.S. Lewis, to whose kindness and critical mind Father Bede professed to owe much.

5

A Venture in Faith

C.S. Lewis had entered Magdalen as a fellow and tutor in English literature shortly before Alan Griffiths began his undergraduate course. For two years they had no contact, but after Alan's change of faculty in his third year it was to C.S. Lewis that he had each week to present an essay on some subject in English literature. Since his early teens Alan had been rejecting barren intellectualism in favour of an emphasis on the importance of the imagination. When he first came to C.S. Lewis he brought with him not only the antimoral side of the romanticism he was in, which, as Lewis would remind him in a letter in 1938, meant that in their fiercest arguments Alan would actually defend cruelty and lechery, but also a fervent hostility towards Dryden, Pope and the Age of Reason, and the conviction that it was not through reason but through poetry and imagination that man was fulfilled. There was about the fervour of this conviction an almost religious quality and indeed it is probably true to suggest that for Alan Griffiths at that time religion was nothing and the romanticism he expounded was his religion. In a paper which he prepared for a literary society over which Lewis presided he even went so far as to suggest that what was needed was a new religion of which Wordsworth, Shelley, Keats and the other leaders of the Romantic movement were the prophets. The love of nature was after all the only thing which moved him deeply and in Wordsworth he found a religion which was wholly based on this.

C.S. Lewis in 1927 was no more of a Christian than his pupil, but he had experienced a similar phase of romanticism, worked through it and come to a more balanced and rational philosophy. At their first meeting when Alan explained his reasons for wanting to read English, Lewis argued strongly against his view, but he must have recognized that the young man was at least prepared to study English literature seriously. One thing which Lewis would not tolerate in his undergraduates was a lack of commitment. He once castigated one young man who produced an essay which was simply copied from a work of criticism so devastatingly that he left Oxford altogether. To those who were at all sympathetic to the subject, however, he was, to use Father Bede's expression, 'wonderful'. For reasons which Father Bede would profess not fully to understand C.S. Lewis took to his new pupil. Perhaps it was that Alan Griffiths became, as he himself suggests might be the case, a foil for Lewis, or perhaps it was that he in fact played a less subordinate role in their relationship than Father Bede would care to imply. Much later in their friendship in one of the letters forming part of what Lewis describes in *Surprised by Joy* as a 'copious correspondence', he would refer to 'Dom Bede' as 'one of the greatest dialecticians of my acquaintance'. Alan Griffiths, for all his anti-intellectual stance, was no doubt able to meet his tutor with creative argument at a very intellectual level. The talks which ensued from Lewis' criticisms of his pupil's essays extended and their acquaintanceship developed spontaneously into a friendship. On one occasion Alan remained talking late into the night and had to run to be out of college before the clock had finished striking twelve for no one was permitted to enter or leave college after midnight. 'Our friendship', Lewis would explain, 'began in disagreement and matured in argument.'

In answer to Alan Griffiths' extreme romanticism Lewis lent him an essay he had just written entitled *Summa Metaphysica contra Anthroposophos* which was his reaction to his friend Owen Barfield who had become a disciple of Rudolf Steiner. Lewis had passed through atheism and had reached the stage of belief in a Universal Spirit, though he still would not call this spirit God. In his essay he outlined his conception of the Universal Spirit behind all phenomena. It was a conception which spoke directly to Alan's need and one to which he inclined even after Lewis had abandoned it. When later Lewis reacted against this 'Universal Spirit' in favour of a personal God on the ground that one could not enter into personal relations with such a conception, his friend would feel that the reaction was too strong. Like Lewis, he recognized the danger of substituting abstract for concrete and personal terms when speaking about God but his own reaction to Lewis' enquiry in *Letters to Malcolm*: 'What soul ever perished for believing that God the Father had a beard?' was that whilst no soul might actually have perished for such a belief, the impoverishment of religious faith due to this and the scandal caused to unbelievers by such childish religious beliefs were as damaging as any liberal theology that might conceal itself in abstractions.

Owen Barfield's *Poetic Diction* was another work which Lewis passed on to Alan in the early days of their relationship and which would have a lasting impact on his life. As a philologist, Barfield showed how a word such as *pneuma* in Greek or *spiritus* in Latin could mean wind or air or breath or life or soul or spirit. From there he went on to demonstrate how, contrary to the common belief which held that man began by using words to denote material things such as wind or air and then progressed to abstract concepts such as life or soul, the original words contained all these meanings. According to Barfield early languages were for this reason rich and suggestive. Only in the course of time were the different meanings distinguished and individual words assigned to them. It is not difficult to perceive why the idea of language progressing from symbols that were profoundly rich and manifold in their meaning to words that were precise but lacking in their earlier poetic quality spoke eloquently to Alan Griffiths. For him it shed light not only on the growth of language but also on the evolution of man: 'We do not progress from a simple materialistic view of life to a more spiritual understanding, but from a rich, complex, global experience of life to a more rational, analytical understanding, in other words from poetry to prose.'

It was the exchange of books and ideas such as this that set the tenor for Alan's whole relationship with Lewis. Alan's first encounter with his tutor had left the overriding impression of extraordinary intellectual power. It was an impression that did not really alter during the ensuing years: 'He was tremendously intellectual but in a very nice way.' C.S. Lewis could be witty and humorous. He was ready to talk about anything but all his conversations were conducted at the highest level. He liked bawdy jokes, drank beer and smoked a pipe almost constantly, cultivating a rather bucolic kind of behaviour and dress, in an attempt to avoid appearing an 'Oxford intellectual': 'He wanted to be an intellectual in a very practical way.' Yet the image he projected remained that of a man of rigorous critical intellect. At least, that was the perception of his friend of many years, although the possibility exists that it was the powerfully intellectual side of Alan Griffiths that so consistently called forth that aspect of C.S. Lewis, or perhaps it was that the younger man's perception of others was simply limited. Lewis' later writings took Alan Griffiths, by his own admission, totally by surprise. He would never have suspected Lewis to be capable of such astonishing psychological insight as he demonstrated in *The Screwtape Letters* or of being able to communicate so effectively with the ordinary reader. Not a trace of the understanding of children that enabled Lewis to write the Narnia books did Alan discern in him in the initial years of their relationship. Lewis was, Father Bede would later be quick to volunteer, so much richer than he appeared on the surface. His books were so much more human than his friend would ever have anticipated. The important thing in Father Bede's eyes was that Lewis remained open: Lewis, the apparently confirmed bachelor in whose professed opinion women were there to cook and housekeep but not to intrude upon the intellectual conversations of men, would thus show himself to be capable of falling madly and happily in love with a woman who was in every way the antithesis of him. Lewis the atheist would become the great Christian writer, Lewis the man of reason would also emerge as the imaginative genius.

The relationship between the world of the intellect and the

world of the imagination was a crucial issue for Lewis. In *Surprised by Joy* he describes how he discovered Siegfried and the *Twilight of the Gods*, and how the world of Norse mythology took possession of his imagination. Later he wrote of how the 'joy' which he experienced in all this romantic literature receded and he came to think that all he had loved in this world of myth was imaginary, while all that he believed to be real was 'grim and meaningless'. This was the period of his atheism during which his mind and his imagination were divided. It was George MacDonald's *Phantastes* that wrought a change in him. The world of imagination became real for him once more. The reading of English literature and the discovery of the religious background to what he read had a tremendous impact upon him and he would write of how *The Dream of the Rood* and the poetry of Langland, whose *Piers Plowman* was the figure of Christ, moved him deeply. A turning point in Lewis' conversion would come when his friends Tolkien and Dyson convinced him that in Christ myth had become history.

With hindsight, Father Bede would be able to discern that one of the prime problems of Lewis' life must have been that of how to reconcile an extraordinarily acute intellect which made him one of the greatest critics of English literature with a no less powerful imagination capable of creating the planetary novels and the Narnia stories. In less personalized terms the issue was a perennial subject of debate between the two men. It was not without a certain personal relevance to Alan Griffiths. Himself possessed of a highly developed intellect, he had experienced and was still experiencing the world to an extraordinary degree through books, and yet when he read he lived the contents in such a way that the emotional and imaginary involvement was tremendous. Dostoevsky moved him to the depths. He suffered with the afflicted of Tolstoy's Russia. He lived the tragedies of Shakespeare and the love affairs in Hardy or Meredith. In imagination he experienced the rich emotional life that seems to have been lacking from his 'real' life. At seventy-nine, Father Bede would still wonder whether this lack was in fact a

serious deficiency for which imagination could not compensate:

> We always feel that real life is through the senses and through
> actual experience but I wonder really whether there isn't
> sometimes a deeper life in the imagination. A great poet like
> Shakespeare experiences in the outer world but he lives it out in
> imagination, and even take the Hebrew prophets – theirs is a
> tremendous imaginative experience of God.

Ironically perhaps, it was an essay which Alan wrote on Sir
Philip Sidney in which he suggested that Sidney's poetry was
better than much Elizabethan poetry precisely because he
wrote from his own experience that highlighted what would
be a continuing difference of opinion between Lewis and his
pupil. Lewis held that poetry had nothing to do with the
poet's personal feelings. It was a view on which he would
subsequently elaborate in his book *The Personal Heresy*. To
Father Bede, however, Lewis seemed to have concentrated
on poetry as an art or a skill and underestimated the aspect of
the unconscious. The imagination, he maintained, as
Coleridge or Wordsworth understood it, was the meeting
place of the conscious and the unconscious, and it was
through the unconscious that the poet was linked not only
with his own personal feelings but also with the experience of
the race, the collective unconscious of mankind. It was for
this reason that the poet had been called a seer, or *rishi* in
Hindu tradition, and was said to be inspired by the Muses.

There were other sustained differences of opinion between
the two men. They argued constantly but their arguments
stimulated a continuous growth and discovery of new things.
It was, according to Father Bede, always Lewis who set the
pace, but his friend was never far behind and in a remarkable
way they always seemed to 'chime together'. After Alan left
Oxford in 1929 they continued to correspond and to meet at
intervals and between that time and 1932 when they were
both undergoing a conversion to the Christian faith, Alan
was probably closer to C.S. Lewis than anyone else was.

On leaving Magdalen, Alan Griffiths had two available
options with regard to his choice of career. One, through his

friend Hugh Fausset, was to review for the *Times Literary Supplement* but when he applied for the job the reception was not unduly encouraging. The feeling was that young people fresh from Oxford were not ready for the post. He was advised first to obtain some experience. The only alternative for which he was qualified was teaching and it was on a career as a schoolmaster that he was about to embark when the opportunity arose to undertake together with his two friends, Hugh Waterman and Martyn Skinner, an 'experiment in common life'. During a number of the university vacations they had stayed together on a farm in the Cotswolds. They had been separated for a while after Hugh and Martyn had left Oxford. Hugh had had a serious illness and Martyn too was unwell so it had been decided that they would winter in warmer climes. In Italy they had spent many hours looking at the Giotto frescos in the Church at Assisi. On their return the prospect of living and working in a town seemed no more endurable to them than it did to Alan Griffiths and the ideal of living in a country cottage in accordance with the rhythm of nature was still with them. By this time, however, it had matured in the sense that they no longer wished to be mere onlookers in the country life they had sampled in their vacations but wanted instead to be more active participants. Their romanticism was gradually being replaced by a more serious commitment to solid labour and to serious study and thought. They wanted to lead a life of extreme simplicity, supporting themselves by their own labours. Hugh and Martyn had private incomes. They would buy a Cotswold cottage and the three of them 'would have all things in common'.

There was, as Hugh Waterman would subsequently point out, nothing original about the course they chose, 'man's need for God or Truth, or Beauty or a more moral way of living being even more urgent than his need to shelter among his fellow men'. What did perhaps make their protest more remarkable was that it was thirty years ahead of many similar protests that would be made against contemporary life. There was an element of escapism in their venture. Its weakness lay, as Martyn Skinner would explain, in the fact that it was 'too much from, and too little to'. There were also inconsistencies, of which they were not unaware, for in rejecting the world of industrialism and mechanization they were going to live, at least in part, on money which derived from that very system. The experience was nonetheless of value in that it forced them to face the problems of human existence, of food and shelter and clothing at their most fundamental level.

Father Bede, in *The Golden String*, would describe how they bought a four-roomed Cotswold cottage without water, drainage or lighting, in Eastington, a hamlet two miles from Northleach. With the help of the occupant of an adjoining cottage they then acquired some land and a couple of cows and supplied milk to the twenty or so other residents of the village. Milking cows was a task which in general Father Bede loved, although to counterbalance his own perhaps slightly idealized recollections of 'placing his head nice and firmly on the flank and feeling the warmth of the animal', possibly other memories of his somewhat less productive relationship with one cow at Eastington should be included. That particular animal refused obstinately and consistently to let him milk her. Water had to be carried from the village tap which froze in winter, vegetables were grown in their own garden and sanitation consisted of an earth closet outside, from which Alan Griffiths used to collect the contents to use as fertilizer. Inside the house the furnishings were kept to a minimum: a kitchen table, some second-hand wheel-back chairs, wooden beds with mattresses stuffed with straw from a nearby farm, coconut matting on the floor and little else to relieve the bare simplicity of the whitewashed rooms. Crockery was provided in the form of a traditional English type of pottery known as slipware by a contemporary at Oxford, Michael Cardew, whose work would afterwards be exhibited in the Victoria and Albert Museum; and Barbara Griffiths was at one stage enlisted to weave on a loom very rough vests out of wool straight from some Scottish sheep. To what seems to have been an exceptionally accepting family Alan Griffiths' decision to follow Oxford with such rustic living was 'interesting'. His understanding mother took it all in her stride.

Together the three men lived the rhythm of nature, rising

with the dawn, watching the movement of the constellations at night. They steeped themselves in the traditions of the past, shunning such innovations as a gramophone or a wireless. Travel, on the occasions for example when they visited their families, was undertaken on foot, bicycle or horse and cart, for trains were condemned as destroyers of the natural peace and order of the countryside. Entertainment took the form of singing sitting round the kitchen table or reading the literature of the sixteenth or seventeenth centuries or earlier. The books read often by the light of tallow dip candles during that period at Eastington would lead Alan Griffiths from a special attraction to the history and the literature of the seventeenth century as 'a time of violent conflict when all the forces which were to shape modern history were coming into being, but also a time when the traditional order of life was still preserved', to a closer scrutiny of the religion of men such as Hooker and George Herbert whose faith, he began to see progressively more clearly, underlay the whole of their culture. Each equipped with a Black Letter edition of the Authorized Version, Martyn and Hugh and Alan began to read the Bible daily, seated at the kitchen table while the porridge for breakfast was cooking on the fire. Such reading began because of literary interest, as part of the tradition of seventeenth century prose they all loved. For Alan it was the beginning of what would become a daily routine of reading a chapter of the Old Testament and a chapter of the New Testament over the next few years.

The correspondence with C.S. Lewis continued. While Alan was at Eastington Lewis was engaged in an altercation with Owen Barfield, the anthroposophist, which entailed the exchange of essays. Alan Griffiths in the Cotswold cottage shared in the exchange. It was Lewis who had advised Alan on leaving Oxford to read some philosophy to compensate for not having read Greats. Alan read Descartes, Spinoza, the *Meditations* of Marcus Aurelius. Descartes did not appeal to him greatly. Father Bede would never be able to accept that the mind was a pure spirit and the body a pure and separate mechanism, although as a young man he probably did not fully appreciate the implications of the theory that the mind and the body were two perfectly separate substances and he did admire Descartes' capacity to ignore what had gone before and think everything out anew. In Spinoza, on the other hand, Alan found a philosopher after his own heart, a man who valued wisdom above fortune, fame or honour. By this time, it seems, Alan was reacting sufficiently against his own romanticism to respond to the rigidly mathematical approach of Spinoza. He was touched too by the clarity and precision of his style and by his 'moral earnestness'. The analysis of the emotions and the idea that it is by gaining an 'adequate idea' of emotions that freedom from their control is achieved rang a special chord of recognition in Alan Griffiths. It was not, he realized, by evading his passions or suppressing them that he could be free from their influence. It was through self-knowledge that self-control was achieved. This was, although doubtless more readily grasped intellectually than actually practised, the next step on the path to which Lawrence had introduced him. Again, Spinoza's conception of the 'intellectual love of God' met a very specific need in Alan Griffiths. Unconsciously or perhaps half consciously, he was seeking rational evidence for the existence of that which he had experienced in the presence of nature during his last term at school. Spinoza enabled him to subject what had hitherto been but a confused intuition of a deeper reality behind the face of nature to rational scrutiny. 'Spinoza', Father Bede would write in *The Golden String*:

> showed me that the power behind the universe was a rational power, and that to know this reason of the universe was man's highest wisdom. But more than this. This reason of the universe could not only be known but also loved. To accept the order of the universe with one's will; to identify oneself with the will of God was the source of happiness.

Freedom of will consisted of the choice between following the will of God willingly or unwillingly. The logic of what might seem an unduly severe creed appealed to Alan, as did Marcus Aurelius' idea that virtue was its own reward, and that 'to be virtuous was to live according to the reason, the law of the universe, of which our own reason was a part, and a virtuous act was simply an action which was according to nature like the growth of fruit on a tree'.

It was possible to perceive in Alan Griffiths' first readings of philosophy a confirmation and the discovery of a more rational basis for what he had already come to believe through the vital experience of the senses and the imagination. Berkeley's *Principles of Human Knowledge*, however, were to have an even more momentous impact. Alan was attracted both by the style (always for him a not inconsiderable factor) and by the thought of Berkeley which evoked in him the recognition that it was not possible to conceive of things existing without a mind to know them, that things were essentially ideas of that universal mind or Spirit of the universe with which he was already familiar through Marcus Aurelius and Spinoza. Berkeley, though, did not, like Spinoza, confuse the universe and God by claiming that extension was an attribute of God, a fact which Alan appreciated: 'God was a mind, a pure Spirit, and the universe was the thought of his mind, while our own perception of things was simply a limited participation, as Marcus Aurelius had held, in the mind or reason of God.'

The real breakthrough derived from the fact that the concept of an eternal Spirit, which was one with which Alan Griffiths could reconcile his own experience of a Presence in nature, was one advocated by a bishop of the established Church. For the first time it came to him that his own experience might have some link with the God of orthodox Christianity. Though still very far from accepting Christian doctrine, from this point onwards his mind became more open. He read the *Confessions* of St Augustine primarily for their literary interest and in the original, because when he mentioned his intention of reading them C.S. Lewis had assumed he meant in the language in which they were first written. Alan Griffiths rose to the challenge with a struggle but thereafter he would always make a point of reading works in their original no matter how scant his knowledge of the language. The effort involved would, he felt, bring him into more vital contact with the mind of the author. In the case of the *Confessions*, the contact with St Augustine filled the reader with a degree of emotion which previously only Shelley and Swinburne had been able to evoke in him. Yet it was not now the vague emotionalism of Swinburne that so aroused him but the intense religious love of a great Christian saint whose idea of God was real and rational in a way that could not fail to speak to Alan Griffiths. 'Here was in fact', Father Bede would write in *The Golden String*, 'what I had so long desired to find, a record of a personal experience of passionate intensity and immense imaginative power, engaging all the energies of the intellect and the will in the search for truth.'

Nevertheless, when he embarked upon the reading of Dante it was still with the idea that Christianity was not something of direct relevance to his own position in the contemporary world. The background to *The Divine Comedy*, hell, purgatory and paradise, was as much a piece of mythology to him as their antecedent, the descent of Aeneas into the underworld. Yet the reading of Dante was to mark a significant step in his life. As a poet Dante seemed to him to be far above any other he had read and the greatness of his poetry Alan attributed to the great 'moral and intellectual power of his mind'. Hitherto he had rejected morality as a cold denial of the fire of love and passion, but Dante brought him to the realization that a disciplined and controlled love was stronger and deeper than a love that was given free rein. Until now Shakespeare's heroes had seemed to him to demonstrate the deepest level of human experience but Hamlet, Lear, Macbeth, Antony were all in different ways the victims of their own passion. The key to their tragedy lay in the surrender to it. What Dante revealed to Alan Griffiths was that in the victory over passion there was something greater than tragedy. The *Purgatorio* left him with the conviction that moral virtue was the transformation of passion and not its suppression. Furthermore, it was as impossible for him to disregard the fact that behind the creativity of Dante, as behind that of Giotto and Bach whose work he also held in supreme esteem, there existed 'the massive power of a religion which did not cramp the powers of man but on the contrary developed them to their highest point'.

This then was the prelude and the backcloth to Alan's reading of the Bible in the small cottage at Eastington. Lewis in the Trinity term of 1929 had undergone his first conversion to theism. He had finally given in and 'admitted that God was God'. Alan had not yet reached that stage but the relationship and the debate continued to flourish interrupted only by one very practical hiccup. One weekend Alan was under the impression that Lewis had agreed to come and see the three residents of the cottage in Eastington. They got in some 'visitor's food', to supplement their own very simple diet of vegetable stews, cheese and eggs, and they waited. Alan in particular was in a state of eager expectation, refusing to go for walks unless he felt tired and insisting that he must be fresh to receive the friend whom he considered to have the most exact and penetrating mind he had ever encountered. Lewis never came. It had all been a misunderstanding in the first place and there was no telephone to rectify the situation.

Alan Griffiths did not keep Lewis' early letters, it having not yet occurred to him that his former tutor would become a 'great man' (although his letters from the early 1930s onwards would remain, at least in photocopied form in a cupboard in Father Bede's hut at Saccidananda Ashram), and Lewis did not keep Alan's, and so in later life Father Bede would be uncertain of precisely how close their experience was, although there would be no doubt in his mind that the two men's reading had been along the same lines. For himself, he approached the Bible as he had approached Chaucer, Spenser, Shakespeare, Milton, Wordsworth, Coleridge and a multitude of others. Yet the fact remained that far from seeking mere intellectual stimulus he was looking for a way of life. Oxford had left him with a profound sense of dissatisfaction with the world in which he lived, but it had failed to provide him with a satisfactory philosophy or a definite religion on which to base any alternative. In the Hebrew prophets he discovered a judgement on the modern civilization he condemned, but a judgement based not simply on the fact that it offended against beauty and truth but also on the fact that it offended against the moral order of the universe. In the civilizations of Babylonia and Egypt and in the Greek and Roman Empires he saw the degeneration of a primitive culture to a gross material civilization and the decline of creative energy in the interests of material convenience. He saw now too a breakdown of morality and the enslavement of the poor by the rich, a condition which the prophets, without the kind of moralizing to which he had previously objected, traced to the rejection of God. In the decline of these ancient civilizations he saw reflected his own contemporary world and for the first time began to see its error in terms of its deliberate rejection of the authority of God. In St Paul's Epistle to the Romans too Alan Griffiths perceived a condemnation of his own civilization. St Paul's condemnation of the pagan world possessed of all the vices that Alan had recognized at Oxford was based on the idea that 'knowing God, they glorified him not as God, neither gave thanks, but became vain in their reasonings and their senseless heart was darkened'. St Paul offered a more profound insight into the problem which had concerned Alan at university where many had reacted against conventional Victorian morality by succumbing to irreligion and immorality – that of the choice between immorality and inhuman, loveless morality. St Paul's idea of a love that was a gift of God and a means of transcending the limitations of human love was not so far from the understanding of love Alan had been pursuing in his way of love and imagination. Nor was St Paul's understanding of faith very different from Alan's theory of the imagination as 'the power to see beyond the phenomenon, to grasp that reality which underlies the appearances of this world'. From this recognition it was only a short step to the doctrine of original sin. Not only was modern civilization corrupt, but all the civilizations of the past revealed the same tendency. St Paul showed him that this was related to something in the very nature of man. The world was evil and in a state of sin. Offset against this was the hope of another life in Christ.

' "As in Adam all die",' he wrote to Lewis at that time,

' "even so in Christ shall all be made alive".' Alan had recognized clearly the fact of the solidarity of mankind, that all men together made one man and that Adam, whom St Paul describes as the 'type of him who was to come' was representative of all mankind and was a kind of myth or symbolic figure of whom Christ was the fulfilment. For Lewis the same understanding, together with the recognition that in Christ the myth had become history, was a crucial step in his conversion to Christianity. For Alan it led on to a new appreciation of the Church which until now he had regarded merely as a social institution. All men inherited a nature with a tendency to evil. All received the promise of a new nature in Christ. The Church was this new humanity. 'It was a social order indeed, but it was an order that transcended this world, that is to say, all human civilization. It was a social organism of which Christ was the "head" and all men were potentially its members.'

In the small country village of Eastington Alan Griffiths' life seemed in some way to come together in a coherent whole. The daily life on the farm and in the cottage mirrored the background both of the poetry of Wordsworth and of many of the Bible stories. The life of the people of the Old Testament became current and in general Alan perceived in the Bible and the Christian faith a new relevance. After a while he found it as 'natural to pray as to read poetry or to walk among the hills'. It was Hugh Waterman who first suggested that they should pray but it was a step which Father Bede would look back upon as almost inevitable.

A reader of *The Golden String* might infer from Father Bede's recollection of the period at Eastington that it was an idyllic episode. His memory is understandably a happy one for the months spent there represent, after all, a significant stage in his pilgrim's progress to religious conversion. Yet in his old age Father Bede would admit that he was inclined to view life as a whole in a very optimistic way and that this tendency might account for his failure to perceive the difficulties and the strains when reviewing his own life. There was indeed serenity and exhilaration and satisfaction in the daily round at Eastington and the give and take of the experience would keep the three men who shared in it in a 'community of thought' for well over fifty years. Indeed despite the fact that their individual lives had since been markedly different, early in the 1980s Father Bede would write that he believed that they were closer in friendship than ever before. It was a belief that Hugh Waterman and Martyn Skinner would wholeheartedly endorse. The fact remains, however, that they were markedly different in character and it is perhaps true to suggest that they were not quite as single-minded in their approach as might at first appear.

Alan Griffiths was an idealist and as Hugh Waterman would later make a point of indicating, at Eastington already some way to being an apostle. The eagerness of his idealism was compulsive, his lucidity was admirable but when seized of an idea, every circumstance of life had to be slotted into his theory, and doubts were swept up like leaves. Generally inspiring in the extreme, there were times when this approach could be most infuriating to a mind such as that of Hugh Waterman which liked to see both sides before making itself up, which sought to see how ideas would work out in practice and preferred to play by ear. Years later the three of them would still laugh about a debate on the 'Simple Life' in which Martyn and Hugh cornered Alan into a theory that the village blacksmith could make an X-ray machine. On the whole his friends would concede, however, Alan had the edge on them. Martyn Skinner remembers Alan as a young man arguing a particular viewpoint with great skill and the enthusiasm born of a sense of the tremendous rightness of what he had just seen late into the night. What cannot always have been easy to accept was that next morning he would appear and, following some interim revelation, argue equally vehemently in favour of an opposite point of view. Alan was not a bigot. He was fundamentally kind and capable of feeling deeply for the poor and the suffering but he was perhaps in his youth a little insensitive, insensitive in a way that would lead him a short while later when visiting Martyn, then a patient in the hospital in Oxford to inquire, 'How are you then, Martyn?'

but then interject before his friend had time to reply, 'Now, about papal infallibility. . .'

Eastington was, according to Hugh Waterman who was perhaps less concerned with the function of the papacy, a tough period intellectually and emotionally. It was also tough physically. Martyn Skinner was very crippled at the time with a bad back which made an already austere life more difficult than it need have been. He could get out at times in a pony and trap. He and Hugh once undertook an expedition by this means from Northleach to Gerrards Cross where the Waterman's home was, stopping at pubs where it was still possible to stable horses. On the whole, however, Martyn's mobility was severely restricted in a way that must have been frustrating. While he was wanting and longing to walk, Alan at that time was only walking for his health and longing to get back to his books. Martyn's immobility also meant that he felt the winter cold acutely, especially the frigidity of the small second room on the ground floor in which they used to study each day for several hours. Perhaps it is indicative that when he came to write *The Golden String* Father Bede would make little mention of such difficulties, despite the fact that he himself was always one who loved heat and loathed cold. He would mention only in passing the physical complaints from which they each suffered on leaving Oxford partly, he felt, in consequence of the state of mental and emotional disturbance caused by their conflict with the world as they saw it.

In his thatched hut at Saccidananda Ashram he would speak more explicitly of his own experience. For some years he suffered very badly from constipation and stomach disorders in a way which with hindsight he would identify as psychosomatic and partially due to repressed sex energies. As a young man, intellectually he had reached the conviction that sex energies could be transformed, that the love instinct could find a more complete expression at another level. In his old age Father Bede would claim that he did not think it was possible to have love in the full sense unless the sex energy was in it but that the choice was then available between suppressing it, indulging it or 'surrendering' and transforming it. The principle of transformation was one which under the influence of Sri Aurobindo and Teilhard de Chardin he would eventually apply to life in general – 'I see life in terms of transformation: matter being transformed into life, life into consciousness and consciousness into divine experience' – and what was of prime importance was that nothing must be left out of the process. If anything was suppressed it could not be transformed. Suppressed sex was always disruptive but if it could be accepted and surrendered in prayer it could be transformed - although often not without a struggle. It was a struggle in which Father Bede would be almost constantly engaged for more than fifty years: 'I would have a very deep friendship with somebody. It was really an immensely deep love. It always started in the spirit and then it became emotional and always the sex element came into it, and how to deal with that was the problem for years and years and years.' The struggle created a tension and through tension, Father Bede would assert, one grows, but the gulf between intellectually grasped theory and integrated practice was a wide one and at Eastington, it is probably true to suggest, Alan Griffiths suffered for it.

Despite a lifestyle which had already become quite spontaneously ascetic, towards the end of the period at Eastington the three men began to think in terms of practising some deliberate acts of mortification. They knelt on the bare stones to pray, not in the relative warmth of the kitchen but in the cold at the back of the house. Alan had begun to read the *Imitation of Christ*, primarily as a sample of medieval prose, but its message found a powerful resonance in him. They began fasting. The food at the cottage, for all its simplicity was fresh and appetizing. Martyn Skinner would many years later claim that he had never enjoyed food as much in his life as he did there, and if Alan Griffiths had a weakness of the flesh it was, in his friend's opinion, a liking for food. The author of *The Golden String* would, whilst recognizing that the fasting they undertook was unwise, claim that he could not stand up to any real deprivation, but in fact the experience appears to have triggered off in him a kind of cycle of austerity, a process of self-indulgence in reverse whereby he would indulge, then indulge more until it became difficult to stop. The urge to restrict his intake of food became compulsive. Yet it was Hugh Waterman who had first suggested that they should fast on Fridays. Nonetheless it was Hugh on whom the extreme and unanticipated austerity of the life told most. He was naturally religious but he was also naturally sociable and it is likely that he had never felt quite the same way as Alan and Martyn did about industrialism. At least he was not quite as wholehearted as they were. It was Hugh who was the first to express his intention of leaving but, valuable as they agreed the experience had been, the breaking up of the life at Eastington was something which they probably all accepted as the appropriate course to follow.

6

'Not that we loved God . . .'

Some time before Alan, Hugh and Martyn left Eastington there had been a plan to move elsewhere to start farming properly with Jim Holtom, the resident of the adjoining cottage. Hugh had initially been very keen on the idea but other plans, to get married, took priority. The sense of belonging to nature formed a close bond between him and his wife Eileen and eventually they would join her father on his farm. Hugh would remain a farmer for the rest of his life and his wife would trudge over the hills with him, knee deep in snow, day after day during the winter blizzards, to cut hay out of the rick to feed outlying heifers. First, however, he returned to Oxford to take his degree and for a while became a schoolmaster. Martyn Skinner also went to live on a farm, taking with him Jim Holtom and his family. He married a girl who had been one of two children who stayed with the three residents of the Eastington cottage. The poems he wrote – the *Letters to Malaya*, *The Return of Arthur*, *Old Rectory* – he sent to Alan Griffiths as they came out and each time they inspired in his friend a renewed enthusiasm for his poetry. Alan valued in it the kind of wit and sparkle which was to be found in an eighteenth century poet like Pope, a liveliness of thought which could be humorous or satirical or sometimes farcical, but what appealed to him most was Martyn's observation of nature, to him reminiscent of that of Wordsworth, which was the original inspiration of Martyn's poetry. Throughout his life Martyn Skinner would retain the habit of a constant observation of the changing moods of nature and his poetry evoked its magic and brought out each detail with extraordinary precision. It was this which Alan used to look for in poetry above everything. It reflected his own great love.

From the time of the *Letters to Malaya* through the *Return of Arthur* to *Old Rectory* Martyn had also developed a critique of the whole system of western civilization and the perils of the industrial system in a way which Father Bede would see as reflecting a more consistent stance than his own. He himself, he would feel, had often wavered and tended to compromise with the system. One other aspect of Martyn's poetry he found particularly striking. Hand in hand with the negative criticism of the modern world there would be a 'constant growth of awareness of the opposite values which Martyn had discovered in the poetry and art and philosophy of the past'. In *Old Rectory* the poet traced this evolution from the point when love of nature impelled him to escape from the town into the country, through the recognition of the disastrous character of western civilization which was preparing its own destruction, to the discovery of something deeper than nature at that juncture when for him religion entered nature:

> *Stream and tree*
> *Retained their old enchantment, cloud and hill*
> *Their beauty, but with that of holiness*
> *Evident too; as when the sunset told*
> *The time on the church clock in hands of gold.*

Asked to provide an appraisal of Martyn Skinner's poetry for the Finzi Bookroom at Reading University, Father Bede would see it as fascinating to observe that his friend's love of nature and art and poetry had led him with a sort of inevitability to religion. Poetry was, he felt, in many ways the most natural approach to religion. Few people realized that the sacred Scriptures of the world were nearly all in the form of poetry. The Psalms, the Song of Songs, the Book of Job, indeed so much of the Bible was poetry. Sir Philip Sidney said of the poet, 'He cometh to you in a story' and Jesus himself came 'teaching in parables'. Similarly the Buddha and Ramakrishna taught by stories. The Koran derived much of its beauty and fascination from the beauty of the Arabic language and the *Rig Veda* was a collection of magnificent poems to the Sun and the Fire, the Dawn and the Night, mirroring all the phenomena of nature. 'Too often', Father Bede would conclude, 'religion has meant the denial of nature and poetry, but when we go to its source we find that they are one.'

Much of Martyn Skinner's insight was conspicuously similar to Alan Griffiths' own, but after Eastington their physical paths diverged. Alan returned to his home where for a while he took a job as tutor to a small boy, a post which allowed him time to continue his reading. In the *Summa Theologica* of Thomas Aquinas he found now the 'complete philosophical justification for Christianity'. He was impressed by the comprehensive mind of St Thomas which had confronted all the most difficult problems with regard to the existence and nature of God and was able to provide a reasoned judgement on them. He discovered too St John Chrysostom and kept up his reading of the Anglican divines of the seventeenth century in whom he admired a piety based on the Bible and the Fathers, expressed in the most impressive prose. Politics seems to have regained a more prominent place in his thinking at this time, but by now however it took the form, not of socialism but of a new Toryism, inspired by a political idea of T.S. Eliot based on seventeenth century ideals. It also happened that his local Member of Parliament was a Tory peer who had encouraged the farming of his own estates and who shared Alan's ideal of a democracy founded on agriculture and something of his vision of a new Toryism which would divorce itself from capitalism and re-establish the old hierarchical traditions based on independent ownership, as far as such traditions were possible within a modern democracy.

It was Bede's *History of the English Church and People* that would cause Alan to look upon the past in a new light, or at least to discover a new dimension to the medieval England he had until this point known only through Anglo-Saxon literature, through Chaucer and through Langland, and so to regard more recent history in a new perspective. Bede's historical record was manifestly the work of a great scholar. It recreated with all the accuracy of personal knowledge the life of the Church in the seventh century and it contained an insight that was for Alan Griffiths a revelation: the English Church had been founded by a Roman pope and the first Archbishops of Canterbury and York had been sent from Rome, the ancient English village churches had once resounded with the rite of the Latin Mass. Alan had been attending communion services regularly in the Church of England. He had even reached the stage of considering the possibility of taking holy orders, yet the idea that the Church of England had once been part of the Roman Church just as England had once been part of the Roman Empire had never previously entered his thinking. Now, for the first time he saw English history take its place in the history of Europe. For the first time he saw the Church of England and the world of Dante and St Thomas as both belonging to medieval Christendom. It was an intellectually satisfying discovery but an otherwise unsettling one.

Alan Griffiths' contact with Roman Catholicism had hitherto been minimal. There had been a Catholic family in New Milton but he had never had any direct association with it, at school a small number of his fellow pupils had been taken to Mass on Sunday mornings, and at Oxford a Catholic undergraduate had been pointed out to him as a point of interest. The prevailing attitude was that Roman Catholicism was something foreign and strange. Even Alan's mother with whom his bond, a bond based on duty and love if not on demonstrated emotion, had been strengthened by the fact that he went regularly with her to communion in the Church of England and who was overjoyed at the thought of her son taking orders in it, once expressed the view that nothing would distress her more than that someone close to her should become a Roman Catholic. It was a view which at the time was shared by countless others. She belonged after all to a generation raised at the end of the nineteenth century when Punch cartoons were viciously anti-Catholic and popular tales of how girls were lured into nunneries and confession was merely a process which licensed repetition of the same sins were rife.

Behind all this was something deeply engrained in the psyche of every Englishman and woman, the national pride and prejudice born of the rift with Rome. With this Alan wrestled as he went on to read Newman's *Apologia pro vita sua*. Alan did not fail to be impressed by Newman. They had in many ways pursued the same path for Newman too had based himself on the Bible, the Fathers and the seventeenth-century Anglican divines. It was Newman whom Barbara Griffiths would recall as being particularly responsible for her brother's conversion to Roman Catholicism, Newman who had so fuelled Alan's enthusiasm that his friend's welfare during that hospital visit paled into insignificance beside the issue of papal infallibility. Yet Newman, with what Alan respected as considerably greater knowledge, had turned to the Church of Rome. Disturbed by this fact, he overcame his own fears sufficiently to attend a morning Mass in the Catholic Church at Newbury only to find that the bells, the incense and the unintelligible words created an atmosphere which 'attracted by its mystery' but 'repelled by its strangeness and uncouthness'. Bewildered, he reached the conclusion that to study Catholicism in Dante or St Thomas was quite a different proposition from experiencing it in its modern practice.

Perhaps it would not be entirely unjust to suggest that his experience in the slums of London a short while later would bring him to a not altogether unrelated realization – that it was one thing to care in the abstract albeit deeply for the socially underprivileged, another to work for them in their midst. A conversation with the Catholic priest at Newbury had done little to allay the fears heightened by Alan's attendance at Mass. A visit to the Principal of Cuddesdon Theological College on the other hand had confirmed a resurgent desire to be reconciled with the Church of England and so, to his mother's delight, Alan began to prepare himself for the ministry in the Church in which he had been baptized and brought up. He applied for entrance into Cuddesdon and it was there that it was recommended that he should have some experience of slum life. So it was that he went to stay at the Oxford Mission in Bethnal Green, London, a city which stood for everything he rejected, but it is doubtful whether he was prepared for the full impact of the venture. The shock of the metropolis was too much for a young man who was already suffering from a certain conflict. The compulsion to fast had become even stronger while he had been living at home in Newbury. When he starved himself he seemed to feel a renewal of spiritual energy. The urge to pray became more powerful with each passing day. Yet offset against this was the fact that he became extremely thin and weak. His sister and friends remarked upon his painful thinness and some tried to persuade him to eat properly but for Alan, to relax seemed in some way to allow his faith to slip away from him. His mother must have observed what was happening but did not interfere. He himself summarized his inner turmoil in terms of a conflict 'between reason and common sense on the one hand, and the spirit of prayer and faith on the other hand'.

London intensified the conflict. There was respite to be found among the poor of Bethnal Green and a reminder of the countryside he loved in the produce on the market stalls but the 'world' in the form of the kind of civilization he abhorred seemed to him to be closing in upon him and driving out the spirit of prayer. The cathedrals and the art galleries of the city brought no peace. The people with whom he was staying, though kind, would not have understood his difficulties. Stricken with a profound sense of isolation he knelt on the floor beside his bed and sought repentance in a night of prayer. Some words in a book by Bishop Ken, one of the non-juring bishops of the seventeenth century, on the theme of the need for repentance had awakened in Alan the recognition that he needed to repent. C.S. Lewis would some years later remind his former pupil that: 'What started you off was the consciousness of sin in some religious writer you were reading which you could not share tho' you were satisfied on objective grounds that you were more sinful than the writer.' The precise nature of his sin was initially unclear to Alan Griffiths but he was aware that reason, his own will and his ego had hitherto shaped his religion. 'It had engaged my mind and imagination, my feelings and my will', he would write in *The Golden String*, 'but it had never really touched my heart.' Dimly he must have perceived the need to 'let go', to accept from the heart an authority higher than his own will, but the conflict between reason and faith was not as yet resolved. The fasting and now the call to repent, even the determination to pray through the night, were irrational impulses against which his reason rebelled. In the solitude of his room he struggled for hours until he fully recognized that he must surrender himself to a power with which he could not reason and which presented itself to him at that time as nothing but darkness. During the last hours of the night he seemed to have no alternative but to place himself beside Christ in the Garden of Gethsemane. When he rose from his knees in the morning, he was exhausted and at a loss as to what he should do with his life.

'Retreat' was an expression with which Alan Griffiths was barely familiar. Yet in his state of hopelessness it came to him as if from a source independent of himself that he must go to a retreat. At a retreat for a group of ordinands to which he was referred after consultation at a nearby Anglo-Catholic church, he heard an elderly priest talk on the doctrines of original sin, redemption, the incarnation and the Holy Trinity. The old man based his talk on the teachings of St Thomas, with which Alan was already familiar, but it was the first time that he had heard them given a living personal application, and for the first time they touched his heart. In a flood the repentance which he had sought to no avail the night before rushed over him. He had, he now recognized, rejected the Church and worked out his own religion and here all the time the truth had been among the people to whom he had thought himself superior. Tears poured from him as he made his confession for the first time and when he went into the church and heard the chanting of the 119th Psalm, the words 'With my whole heart have I sought thee: O let me not wander from thy commandments. Open thou mine eyes, that I may behold wondrous things out of thy law,' they seemed to him the articulation of his own prayer. Afterwards when he emerged from the church it was to him as if he had been granted new vision. The streets and buildings of London no longer seemed to bear in upon him. They had somehow lost their solidity. Beyond the hard casing of exterior reality he seemed to perceive the inner being of all that surrounded him: 'I was like a bird which has broken the shell of its egg and finds itself in a new world; like a child who has forced its way out of the womb and sees the light of day for the first time.' Alan Griffiths had made his step into the dark and in doing so had discovered a new experience of love, a love which was as real and personal as any human love could be and yet which transcended human limitations. The words of St John: 'Not that we loved God but that he loved us' assumed a new significance in the light of the realization that in all the experiences which he had looked upon as steps in his ascent to God: the presence which had suggested itself to him beneath the forms of nature that day at school, the beauty he had discovered in the poets, the truth which philosophy had brought to him and the revelation of Christianity; in all these God had in fact been seeking him. He had always suspected that in love the secret of life was to be found. He could imagine no ecstasy of love beyond what he experienced that evening.

Looking back on what took place during the night of prayer and ensuing day Father Bede would perceive in it an experience closely bound up with the imagination. The Book of Common Prayer was very poetic. Plainchant, the Old English of the psalms and of prayers such as 'Lighten our darkness we beseech thee, Oh Lord' appealed to him tremendously for he was, as he would put it, 'living on that level'. Yet it was also an experience in which the mind and the imagination came together and he was able in some sense to 'go beyond'. A short while later this sense of there being a region beyond in which he belonged was to be further reinforced. Returning to Newbury after only a few weeks in London in the conviction that his difficulties were over, he found instead that not only was his passion for fasting more urgent but also that each time he tried to go to bed, the desire to spend the night in prayer would make itself strongly felt. The Cowley Fathers in Oxford, through whom Alan Griffiths had come into contact with a form of Anglo-Catholicism which touched his heart, were unable to provide him with advice which he found useful. The Bible had begun to lose its meaning for him, and so he turned to the mystics. What he read in the mystics encouraged him to believe that the presence which he felt in the depths of his soul was indeed the presence of God, but the sense of infinite power and love of which he was so acutely conscious made it almost impossible for him to make decisions for himself. He needed some form of guidance on which he could depend. Instead he found only confusion. Eventually he decided that he must make a completely new start. Inspired by the life of St Antony, the first hermit of the Egyptian desert, by St Basil and St Gregory of Nazianzus, and almost certainly also by his own innate love for the countryside, Alan set out once more for the Cotswolds in search of a lonely desolate spot in which he could lead a life of prayer and meditation in the hope that God's will for him would be revealed.

From his previous stay in the Cotswolds he recalled a thatched cottage which he thought would make an ideal hermitage but to his dismay discovered on reaching it that it had already been let. Another similar cottage further up the wooded hillside was made available to him by a local farmer and, equipped with the bed and straw mattress which he had used at Eastington together with a sleeping bag, table, stool and clock, he began a life of extreme simplicity in its two otherwise unadorned rooms. It was a lifestyle not dissimilar to that at Eastington but this time his two friends were not present to temper his craving for fasting and a rigorous routine of prayer. When first he arrived a farm labourer and his wife who occupied an adjoining cottage undertook not only to do his laundry but also to provide him with food. At midday he was supplied with some hot vegetables. Otherwise he resolved to live on bread and milk and dried fruit. It was not long before he decided that the hot midday meal was an unnecessary luxury and there came a point where he was living virtually on raw turnips and other vegetables alone. Recreation was reduced to a short afternoon walk in order to extend the time for reading and, above all, for prayer. In the context of this demanding regime the Bible recovered its potency for Alan Griffiths and the conflict between the urge to pray for long hours and the fear of becoming unbalanced was intensified. For two or three months he lived without finding any real peace until finally, despairing of the whole experiment, he wrote to Martyn Skinner asking him to come and collect him and his few belongings.

Having posted the letter, however, it came to him that he was once more taking the direction of his life into his own hands and that he should instead be turning unreservedly to God. He determined then to do what an irrational impulse had for some time been urging him to do, namely to pray without any limitations of time or energy. In a small closet with only a skylight for illumination, he placed himself in imagination at the foot of the cross and immediately felt himself swept up in a great wave of prayer. From eight in the morning until four in the afternoon he prayed, completely unconscious of the passage of time, and when finally he rose from his knees he was aware only that he must not try to live in the manner in which he had been doing but that he should try to work on the farm. He was conscious too that he had in those interim hours in some mysterious way entered into a region beyond all thought or feeling or imagination, a place at the very centre of his being where at times the soul might be in direct contact with God, and that it was to that place that he was powerfully drawn. It was a crucial juncture in his life. Thereafter he would never lose the sense of belonging in that region beyond. In times of difficulty or pain it would diminish in some degree but it would never leave him altogether and it was on the strength of it that he lived.

Next day, in more complete surrender, he took work on the farm and began to eat his meals at the farmhouse with the farmer and his family. A second letter to Martyn Skinner that previous afternoon had cancelled the request for him to come, and so Alan resumed on the 800 acres of farmland the kind of life in harmony with nature and with country people which he had always found compatible with his understanding of the Bible. Still reading much, on free afternoons he would go to Winchcombe to buy books. There he also renewed his friendship with Michael Cardew and it was the former provider of slipware for the Eastington cottage who introduced Alan to the only woman he ever considered marrying. Alan had had other female friends, some of them quite close. At least he did not share the attitude of his friend, C.S. Lewis who in May 1943 would write congratulating his 'dear Dom Bede' on an article he had written on friendship: 'The decay of friendship, owing to the endless presence of women everywhere, is a thing I'm rather afraid of.'

Nevertheless, the closeness Alan had experienced had been based on the fact that he had found them 'very interesting people' and his relationship with Barbara Millard, for all his consideration of marriage, was probably not so very different. She was a South African who had been brought up in Southern Rhodesia. She was a keen horsewoman and she shared Alan's love for the open country. Together they went on walks and picnics. Together, too, they went to communion at the church in Winchcombe. Alan was troubled about the doctrine of the Church of England with regard to the true nature of the sacrament of communion. The fact that the Church of England embraced several views, that there were those who saw the sacrament as the Body of Christ, others who felt that Christ was simply present in some undefined way, and yet others who held that it was merely bread and wine which faith transformed into a means of communion with Christ, disturbed him. Barbara Millard also had her difficulties with the Church of England and they spent many hours in deep discussion on the subject. Yet, as Alan himself recognized, it remained more a relationship of friendship, albeit friendship founded on the love of God, than of the kind of love between a man and woman that more usually leads to marriage. Barbara Millard returned to South Africa where she married. For several years she kept in touch with her friend in England by letter until, one day, he received news from her husband that she had been killed by a fall from her horse. Inevitably the news came as a shock but there was consolation for Alan in the conviction that theirs had been the kind of relationship which unites two individuals in such a way that death itself cannot divide them. The relationship with Barbara had surprised his friends. Marriage, they felt, for Alan would be a grave mistake, and it was not something that would ever enter into his thinking again.

Despite his difficulties with certain aspects of Church of England doctrine, Alan had not returned to a serious consideration of Roman Catholicism since the explorations that followed his first encounter with Newman's *Apologia pro vita sua*. When, having seen an advertisement in a catalogue for Newman's *Essay on the Development of Christian Doctrine*, he went out and bought a copy it was 'simply out of general interest'. Nevertheless, its effect on him was to prove decisive. His sympathy with Newman was based on the recognition that theirs had been a common approach to the Church, via the Bible, the Fathers and the High Church, on a respect for his powers of exegesis, and on the fact that the perspective which Newman offered on the Church was an historical one. Each day Alan Griffiths worked beside the other men on the farm topping turnips; each evening he would return to his cottage to read more of Newman. He already believed that the Church which Christ had founded was an historical reality, 'that it had had a continuous history from the time of the Apostles to the present day'. In his book, written hardly coincidentally only a few years after Darwin's *Origin of Species*, Newman offered him the vision of a Church, the Mystical Body of Christ, as a living organism with a gradual organic development from small beginnings to much greater dimensions, an organism with an inner principle of growth like any other and capable, like any other, of false developments and failures of adaptation. Papal authority, the doctrines of purgatory and indulgences, of the cultus and the saints and their relics – all of these disputed teachings Newman showed to be organic developments of the original doctrine of the gospel by the same principle that transformed an acorn into a mighty oak. The tests which Newman, a man not originally inclined to the view he found himself expounding, applied with scientific exactitude to determine the genuineness of the development, did not fail to impress his reader. 'I had sought', Father Bede would write in *The Golden String*

> to find in the Church of England the living representative of the Church which Christ had founded. Now I saw that the living Church which could show a continuous evolution from the day of Pentecost and whose doctrine had been built up through successive centuries through the guidance of the indwelling Spirit, was none other than the Church of Rome.

It was once more to the bookseller in Winchcombe that Alan resorted for information as to the whereabouts of the nearest Roman Catholic church. He was directed to a church just round the corner. The parish priest, a Father Palmer, was on this occasion a man with whom Alan could establish an immediate rapport. Father Palmer had nearly been sent to school at Christ's Hospital but his mother, on discovering that her son would have to attend a Protestant service, had responded that she would rather take her eleven children to the workhouse than have him subjected to such an experience. Conscious to some degree, although as he would reflect in later life not fully, of the hurt that he would cause his own mother by joining a Church she viewed with such suspicion, Alan wrote to her at that time that he would do nothing until he was positively assured of the presence of Christ in the Church. In the interim Father Palmer lent him two books, *Christ in the Church* and *The Friendship of Christ*, both by R.H. Benson, and in the course of conversation one day he mentioned casually to Alan that he should go and visit the Prior of Prinknash Priory.

7

Prinknash and the Monastic Life

If, until now, the presence of God had revealed itself most poignantly to Alan Griffiths in the mystery of nature, the Benedictine monastery of Prinknash to which Father Palmer took him would reveal to him the presence of God in what he described as 'Grace'. It was true that Prinknash Priory, as it was then, was possessed of a natural beauty to which Alan did not fail to respond. Nestling on the side of one of the wooded slopes between Gloucester and Cheltenham, the old Cotswold manor house that had become the home for a community of some thirty monks looked out over fields studded with trees and a plain stretching away to the distant Malvern hills. There was external beauty too in the music of the choir, in the white habits of the monks and in the rhythm and dignity of their life together, but this, Alan now recognized, was but the outer manifestation of a beauty of a supernatural order, the secret of which, he began to perceive, was prayer.

Despite his own experience of the powerful urge to pray, the atmosphere at Prinknash, in which prayer was as natural a part of existence as taking breath and in which the supernatural world was a readily accepted background to everyday life, was something totally new to him. Indeed the whole idea of monastic life in the contemporary world came to him as something very novel. If he had previously encountered it at all it had been in the form of the ruins of Rievaulx or in the course of his reading of Chaucer. To him monasteries belonged very much to the past. Yet Prinknash impressed and attracted him. In a way it represented the answer to what he had long considered to be the problem of the modern world, a world empty and devoid of meaning because it was cut off from its source in God. For its part, the community received him with sensitivity and understanding. Prinknash was a Benedictine monastery originally founded in the Church of England in an attempt to restore the monastic life within that Church. Only after having for some years failed to find any authority for its way of life in the Church of England was it received into the Catholic Church. It had remained tolerant and open. The Prior at the time, Father Benedict Steuart, recognizing in the young visitor uncommon potential but not uncommon difficulties, handled him with wisdom and kindness. Alan had been through a very demanding period physically, mentally and spiritually. Excessive fasting had made him both thin and overwrought. The Prior invited him to remain at Prinknash for as long as he wished and ordered him to eat whatever was put in front of him. For six weeks he stayed, during which time he attended the Offices and had free access to the books in the library. He received no formal religious instruction but Father Benedict Steuart made himself available after dinner in the refectory to answer his questions on prayer, on theology and on a subject which was treated with a naturalness which Alan particularly appreciated, sex.

With each passing day the conviction grew that at Prinknash he had found both the truth, and equally importantly, the life he had been seeking. In the balance of prayer and work undertaken in the monastery garden, the farm and the carpenter's shop, and especially in the spirit of kindness, hospitality and charity that pervaded everything, he identified the sign, for which he had told his mother he would wait. The spirit of charity was to him the visible evidence of the presence of Christ in the Church. At Prinknash, on Christmas Eve 1932, he was received into the Catholic Church by Father Benedict Steuart, and at Midnight Mass he made his first communion in the village church at Winchcombe.

No member of his family was present at the ceremony that Christmas Eve. He had lived apart from them for a good time and though they were all friendly and though his second brother in particular, who was a high Anglican, very much appreciated what he was doing, none of them were very close to him at the time. He himself saw his conversion very much in terms of the Gospel text: 'Unless a man will hate his father and his mother and his wife and his children, and his own life also, he cannot be my disciple.' Alan Griffiths did not fail to recognize in these words the deliberate force of paradox which warned that they were not to be taken too literally, but at the same time he knew that they were meant to present a challenge to worldly values and he was ready to rise to that challenge – perhaps just a little more easily than the greater sensitivity which came with advancing years would have permitted. In his old age he would acknowledge that he had failed fully to appreciate the extent of his mother's pain at the 'loss' of a favourite child who had passed so successfully through his schooling and Oxford. At the time Alan was fired with all the enthusiasm and evangelistic ardour of the new convert, so much so that C.S. Lewis was induced to insist quite forcefully that he must desist from trying to convert him. They were still close. The same year in which Alan became a Catholic he had been on a walking tour with Lewis and his friend, Owen Barfield. They had both come to religion through books, both, as Lewis wrote to him in April 1936, 'chiefly by Reason' (though he added the swift proviso 'I don't mean, of course, that any one comes at all but by God's grace – I am talking about the route not the motive power'), and they had taken many steps along that route together, but this last was one which Lewis did not feel that he could share. Lewis was not without tolerance in his attitude. In fact it was from a vantage point of greater tolerance that he at times argued with the newly Catholic Alan Griffiths. 'Is it not held that many who have lived and died outside the visible Church are finally saved because Divine Grace has guided them to concentrate solely on the true elements of their religion?'

Lewis reasoned thus in a letter written shortly after Alan entered Prinknash to try his vocation as a monk, only months after his entry into the Roman Church. He was arguing against the right to pray for the conversion of other people and the tenor in which the letter continues suggests that more specifically he was indicating his own lack of receptivity to his friend's sense of the terrific rightness of what he had discovered:

> And while I am on the subject, I had better say once and for all that I do not intend to discuss with you in future, if I can help it, any of the questions at issue between our respective churches. It would have the same unreality as those absurd conversations in which we are invited to speak frankly to a woman about some indelicate matter – which means that she can say what she likes and we can't. I could not now that you are a monk, use that freedom in attacking your position which you undoubtedly would use in attacking mine. I do not think there is anything distressing for either of us in agreeing to be silent on this matter: I have had a Catholic among my most intimate friends for many years and a great deal of our conversation has been religious. When all is said (and truly said) about the divisions of Christendom, there remains, by God's mercy, an enormous common ground.

Yet Lewis was, after all, an Ulsterman and the younger man's enthusiasm was, as Father Bede would subsequently volunteer, excessive. It was this desire to communicate the truth he had discovered that had induced him first to consider becoming a Franciscan or a Dominican. Before committing himself to the Benedictines he spent time with both of these other Orders without really feeling that they were for him, until Father Benedict Steuart suggested to him that since God had sent him to Prinknash that might be where he was intended to remain. Only slowly did it dawn on him that it might be possible to follow Christ without becoming a preacher and that a significant part of the life of Christ had been spent, not in teaching but in quiet obscurity among the village people of Nazareth. The desire to share the thrill of his discoveries with Lewis persisted but though they remained friends and though they continued to correspond until Lewis' death, following Alan's entry into the Roman Church a certain barrier seems to have fallen between them. As Lewis wrote shortly after a visit to Prinknash in December 1934:

If you are going to argue with me on the points at issue between our two churches it is obvious that you must argue *to* the truth of your position, not *from* it. The opposite procedure only wastes your time and leaves me to reply, moved solely by embarrassment, *tu sei santo ma tu non sei filosofo*! [You may be holy but you're no philosopher!]

By 1936 the differences in belief, despite such protestations, were still the subject of debate. Alan, in one of his letters to Lewis had evidently written: 'You have no reason to fear that anything you say can have any serious effect on me.' Lewis' response was:

The underlying assumption that anyone who knew you would feel such a fear is not only funny but excruciatingly funny . . . ask the Prior if he sees the joke: I rather think he will.

As to the main issue I can only repeat what I have said before. One of the most important differences between us is our estimate of the importance of the differences. You, in your charity, are anxious to convert me: but I am not in the least anxious to convert you. You think my specifically Protestant beliefs a tissue of damnable errors: I think your specifically Catholic beliefs a mass of comparatively harmless human tradition which may be fatal to certain souls under special conditions, but which I think suitable for you. I therefore feel no *duty* to attack you: and I certainly feel no *inclination* to add to my other works an epistolary controversy with one of the toughest dialecticians of my acquaintance, to which he can devote as much time and reading as he likes and I can devote very little. As well – who wants to debate with a man who begins by saying that no argument can possibly move him? Talk sense, man! With other Catholics I find no difficulty in deriving much edification from religious talk on the common ground: but you refuse to show any interest except in differences.

It was not, Father Bede would some years later explain, that he had really wished to convert Lewis to Catholicism any more than he had wished to convert him to Christianity. It was simply that he wanted to continue the debate between them and in doing so to learn from Lewis as he had done in the past. The remark that Lewis had found so 'excruciatingly funny' had been intended only to suggest that Alan's actual faith would not be influenced by anything Lewis said, but possibly Alan's attitude had changed more than he himself realized and undoubtedly he was somewhat too anxious to share his understanding of faith. April 1938 would see Lewis once more protesting the pointlessness of exploring their 'differences':

> I feel that whenever two members of different communions succeed in sharing the spiritual life so far as they can now share it, and are thus forced to regard each other as Christians, they are really helping on reunion by producing the conditions without which official reunion would be quite barren. I feel sure that this is the layman's chief contribution to the task, and some of us are being enabled to perform it. You who are a priest and a theologian, are a different story: and on the purely natural and temperamental level there is, and always has been, a sort of tension between us two which prevents our doing much mutual good. We shall both be nicer, please God, in a better place.

The agreement not to discuss such differences upon which the two men finally settled seems to have satisfied C.S. Lewis but as far as his friend was concerned the arrangement introduced a degree of reserve into their relationship. It meant that he must avoid mentioning much that meant more to him than anything else.

The Roman Catholic Church and Prinknash had at last brought to Alan Griffiths a certain peace. It was, Father Bede would reflect in his old age, the one monastery in England where he could really have felt at home: 'The others were too intellectual. Downside, for example, would have ruined me because it would have developed all the intellectual side of me.' By this time he had recognized that he needed something else. Prinknash he found very far from intellectual. It was devotional and liturgical in a way which was for him very salutary. After leaving his family's house in search of a Cotswold hermitage with the feeling that he would not ever return home, Alan Griffiths would never again touch a piano but his sensitivity to music and the arts would not leave him. In the plainchant of the monastery's worship he recognized an art form which had not in any way become separated from religion. Indeed, its sole purpose was to raise the heart and mind to God in prayer. To participate in the liturgy was, as he would explain in *The Golden String*, 'to share mystically in the life and death and resurrection of Christ, to receive the gift of the Spirit at Pentecost and to participate in the communion of the saints'. In the architecture and ornament-ation of the church, the music and movement of the ceremony, all the arts combined to perform their highest function. They became the concrete embodiment of the mystery of the divine Word at the centre of which was the daily Mass. It is not difficult to discern why in a life in which practical action was intimately related to worship in this form Alan should have seen the end of a long search.

If there was any doubt attached to his decision to join the community at Prinknash it was in connection with the fact that the lifestyle did not at first seem rigorous enough for him. Something of this feeling lay at the roots of his decision to spend some time with the Cistercians at Caldey, but, as so often, he had formed a preconceived idea of Cistercian life, through his reading of books. The reality proved to bear not the remotest resemblance to what he had looked forward to: 'It was very like being back in a school room. You had this chair and a desk in front of you and they gave you lessons. It was just the opposite of what I had expected.' After only two days he went to the prior and asked to leave but the prior insisted on his remaining for a week or so to give Caldey a fairer trial. He remained, but in a state of unhappiness, and returned to Prinknash with renewed appreciation. There were no other regrets. He had come to the point where the life which Prinknash offered him seemed the only way. Alone in the Cotswolds he had gradually withdrawn from the world. He needed the balance and support of a human community. In the monastic community Alan identified the pattern of the early Christian community whose members had practised a strict Communism which he found attractive: 'All things were held in common and no one presumed to call anything which he possessed his own . . . and distribution was made to each according to his need.' More than this, Prinknash was a community which would lead him gradually to a more humanistic view of Christianity and of the place of the body, the senses and the feelings. Gradually his psychosomatic illnesses would begin to disappear. If he read St John of the Cross or St Teresa of Avila or when he fasted during Lent his difficulties would return but with the support of the community his balance was more readily redressed. It might even be taken as a tribute to those to whose guidance he was submitted that, on seeing a photograph of his friend taken in 1940, Lewis was able to tease him in a way which must have brought a smile to what Lewis described as his friend's 'Celtic' face: 'You look positively fat in the photograph – you abbey lubber.'

For its part the community was quick to recognize unusual potential. In the words of one who would himself later become abbot of Prinknash, Abbot Dyfrig Rushton: 'From the word go you could see that there was something special about him.' Because he had been received so recently into the Roman Catholic Church Alan Griffiths was given a year's postulancy or trial period instead of the usual six months. He was clothed as a novice on 20 December 1932, when his name was changed to Bede, the saint whose history had made such a profound impact on his life. On 21 December 1933, having been subjected to the three 'scrutinies' held by the council of senior monks at intervals during the year to decide whether a novice is fit to continue and having achieved the necessary two-thirds majority vote of the Chapter, he was allowed to make his simple profession, a vow to observe poverty, chastity and obedience as a member of the community for a period of three years. At the end of that period, his future having once more been put to the vote of all the solemnly professed monks in the community, the Abbot allowed him to make his solemn profession. On 21 December 1936 in what he found a most moving and impressive ceremony, Dom Bede Griffiths made a vow for life according to the Rule of St Benedict 'of stability, conversion of life and obedience'.

His had been a smooth and happy progression to the position of fully professed monk and it would not be long before Father Benedict Steuart's successor, recognizing

Bede's abilities, placed him in charge of studies at Prinknash. As soon as he had made his simple vows he had himself begun to study philosophy in preparation for the priesthood and after his solemn vows he took up theology, not because he had had ordination in mind when first he joined the brothers but because he was drawn to such studies and priesthood was the usual outcome of such a course. 'Priesthood' Father Bede would later define as a ministry to people which, unless an individual has a particular calling to celibacy, may not be incompatible with marriage; a monk's calling was to live in search of God. Even within the confines of the monastery – for fifteen years he hardly went out of the monastery grounds except to go to the dentist – he was not without his 'ministry to people'. Not long after his solemn profession he was appointed guestmaster which meant the encounter with a constant flow of people from all different walks of life and a wide variety of religious backgrounds, and the forming of relationships not merely at the level of superficial social intercourse but at that of the more profound needs of the spiritual life. Nevertheless, when on 9 March 1940, he was ordained a priest by Bishop William Lee of Clifton, it was not, perhaps significantly for one who had so often sought so rationally to control his life, so much as a result of a conscious personal decision as of a natural sequence of events.

Looking back upon those years at Prinknash from his hut in Shantivanam Father Bede presented them as years of untempered happiness: years of a life in which nothing was profane, in which each day from dawn till after dark was set within a round of prayer which gave a sacred character to every activity undertaken, years when together with the other brothers he worked on the monastery farm, in the carpenter's shop and took a hand in building and plastering work, years in a community of 'very nice people' during which the love for others which had never before been able to find an outlet began to fill his whole being. Only when pressed did he acknowledge that there must have been tensions, that the emphasis on obedience in monastic life which had its very positive side had its negative aspects also and that it was only after much painful renunciation that the lesson of humility began to be learnt and the gift of love was given – but then 'life is a struggle you know'.

There were other trials during that period. In 1938, a short while after Dom Bede's solemn profession his mother was involved in a car accident in which one of his brothers had been driving. The brother suffered no permanent injury but his mother never regained consciousness. Father Bede had been separated from his family for some time in terms of both space and thought. The weakening of links with relatives and friends inevitably brought about by entry into monastic life was in his case reinforced by his adoption of the Roman Catholic faith. Kneeling at the hospital bedside of his unconscious mother Dom Bede was aware of a sense of closeness rather than of sorrow. Now the fact that his love for her, never very demonstratively expressed, seemed always to have operated at a higher level served to reinforce the conviction that in dying she would be passing into a region where misunderstanding and separation would have no place, into what he would subsequently describe in *The Golden String* as 'that inner sanctuary of truth and love where one day we would be united for ever'. His father did not die until he was well into his eighties but long before then he had ceased to feature significantly in Father Bede's life.

War in 1939 disrupted even the contemplative life at Prinknash. At the very outbreak an appeal was made to what was by this time an Abbey for chaplains to the Forces. In response every priest in the house volunteered. The Abbot felt bound to restrict the number sent to one for each of the Forces but even so this increased the load of work on those remaining in a diocese expanded by evacuation and bereft of many of its priests. Because an aircraft factory was sited in the vicinity Prinknash was considered to be in a danger zone and a watch had to be kept in the house. The monks also manned the A.R.P. post in the village throughout the war. Father Bede himself would in later life marvel at how completely unscathed his life through two world wars had left him and at how little experience of violence of any kind they had brought him. He took his turn at keeping watch and giving yellow and red warnings, a procedure which he found interesting. Each night at about 11 p.m. German planes would pass over on their way to Coventry and at about 2 a.m. they would return. In the distance he would hear the anti-aircraft guns at Cheltenham opening up. On one occasion he was able to watch quite clearly as a German bomber passed overhead to bomb the aircraft factory at Gloucester. The bomb was dropped, caught only the very edge of its target and the plane turned and disappeared. That was the nearest Dom Bede came to actual contact with the war. Otherwise he was occupied on the farm.

For much of the war he was also busy breaking stones in a local stone quarry. The monks at Prinknash were in need of a larger abbey. In 1939 the foundation stone of a new building on the other side of the estate had been laid by Cardinal Hinsley. Inevitably the war impeded the construction of the new building but a thousand tons of concrete were put into the foundations and Dom Bede amongst others was put to work breaking stones for the new abbey. He became a plasterer and decorator also, and an electrician's mate. It was all very unskilled labour but he enjoyed it nonetheless. Though not quite as inept as Lewis was in that respect, Father Bede professes not to be very good with his hands but he has always seen in manual labour a 'tremendous outlet'. It provided a balance to his studies and his reading. He had by no means abandoned his love of books. For an hour each afternoon the monks had a siesta. During that hour, through-out his time in the monastery, Dom Bede would read a novel. So it was that for an hour a day for several weeks he read *War and Peace* and for that brief daily interval really lived in Tolstoy's Russia.

The years at Prinknash were also the time of the main thrust of his reading of works that would undoubtedly shape his life to come, for it was here that, encouraged to read as widely as possible, he began to study the history of Chinese and Indian philosophy in earnest. It was not his first encounter with some of the classics of Eastern thought. In his exploration of philosophy after Oxford, he had been introduced to the *Bhagavad Gita*, the *Buddha's Way of Virtue* and the *Sayings* of Lao Tzu by a friend of his mother, a theosophist and a suffragette who had carved an indelible impression on his mind as a child by smoking cigarettes. Another of his childhood memories recalls his first experience of Indian people. In the village in Hampshire close to where Alan was living when he was eight or nine there had been an Indian convalescent camp. In a teashop run by two ladies to provide refreshments for these soldiers Alan used to help to serve tea. The Sikhs there used to call the boy their 'little brother', and even did so on one occasion to his mother whose response was a polite but somewhat bemused, 'Oh really'. It was a token of the relaxed nature of their relationship with Alan that they would take their turbans off in front of him. Their warmth and spontaneity, even then, held a special attraction for the boy and for a long time, when he was at school, it was his ambition to join the Indian Civil Service. Later, when he became a pacifist, he was greatly impressed by Mahatma Gandhi. Reading the lives of both Lenin and Gandhi, he could not help but reach the conclusion that Lenin with his belief in violence, materialism and mass organization stood for everything that he disliked, while Gandhi with his faith in non-violence and truth, the village community and the spinning-wheel, stood for all that he admired. In 1931 he had had an opportunity of meeting Gandhi when he came to London to the Round Table conference, but this was the time when Alan had been undergoing his spiritual crisis in Bethnal Green. It prevented him from seeing the Mahatma. Nevertheless Gandhi's conception of life and the spiritual principles which underlay it fixed themselves in his mind. The sense of an ultimate reality beyond the finite world, whether it was called Brahman or Atman or Nirvana, which alone gave meaning to life, would remain with him and in time he would come to see that the only way to reach this reality was by total detachment from this world. At the same time Gandhi brought home to him the idea that detachment was not a way of escape from the world but of a freedom from self-interest which enabled the individual to give himself totally to God and to the world. When, in his early twenties, Alan Griffiths came to read those three great works of eastern wisdom, they did not at the time do much more than provide a wider, non-Christian background to his thinking, although even then he was struck by the fact that he did not find anything unchristian in them. The influence of this eastern thought seems to have lain quiescent in him for some time until a succession of unforeseen circumstances and encounters would lead him to make a deeper study of the spiritual traditions to which they belonged.

It was partly through the reading of Christopher Dawson and partly through the interest of several friends in oriental thought that Dom Bede came to a systematic study of the history of Chinese and Indian philosophy. By Dawson he was shown how throughout the world religion had influenced the pattern of culture not only of all primitive races but also of such splendid civilizations as those of Egypt and Babylonia since the earliest known cultures. Dawson also confirmed his own view of the degradation of society that had so troubled Alan at Oxford by showing how from the tenth century European civilization had been built on the Christian faith until in the eighteenth and nineteenth centuries the idea of secular progress had been substituted for religion as society's guiding principle. Dom Bede himself had begun to see ever more distinctly Catholicism as the source of a new Christian culture which would be able to make use of all the advances of science, but increasingly he recognized that such a new Christian civilization could no longer be of a purely European nature. The Church was now extended throughout the world and people in general were becoming more conscious of Africa and Asia as political and as cultural powers. In Indian philosophy Dom Bede discovered a tradition which went back as far as the very beginnings of Greek philosophy in the sixth century BC, a tradition which like Christian philosophy had developed without a break to the present day. Hinduism was a religion based on a unique experience of

God attained by the *rishis*, which had been transmitted through the *Upanishads* and later the *Bhagavad Gita*, and developed with wonderful resourcefulness through Yoga and the Vedanta for more than 2,000 years. Vedanta, meaning the 'end of the *Vedas*', the philosophy of Hinduism and the supreme wisdom in the light of which the Hindu viewed all philosophies and religion was originally used in the *Upanishads* as the last stage of the *Vedas* in 600 BC, had moved on to the *Bhagavad Gita* in about 300 BC, had been summarized in the *Vedanta Sutras* in about 100 BC and was undergoing a great revival in the modern world. One fundamental difference between Greek and Indian philosophy seemed to Dom Bede of particular significance at this stage: whereas in Greek philosophy man stood at the centre of the universe and everything was regarded in relation to him, in Indian philosophy the supreme reality was Brahman, the absolute Being, and it was in relation to this absolute reality that the transitory world of man and nature was invariably considered.

Dom Bede remained certain that there was only one absolute Way. The Way, the Truth and the Life was Christ, without whom no man came to the Father but he was equally convinced that all religious traditions contained some elements of the truth. Among such non-Christian traditions it was always Hinduism that particularly attracted. Buddhism he studied only in a 'rather roundabout way' although his interest in Tibetan Buddhism would develop in later years, but the Vedanta interested him from the very first, and evidently, even before they had both become Christians, he and Lewis had reached the conclusion that the 'fullness' of religion was to be found either in Christianity or in Hinduism. 'You will remember', wrote Lewis in one of his letters, 'that long ago you and I agreed, being still unbelievers, that Hinduism and Christianity were the only two things worth serious consideration. I still think it was a sound decision.' Yet the same letter concludes: 'I no longer want to read Eastern books: except good non-religious books like Confucius.' Lewis was of the opinion that Hinduism was 'neither of divine nor diabolical origins but profoundly and *hopelessly* natural', but Lewis never really subjected Hinduism to very close scrutiny. Father Bede felt sure that as an anthroposophist Owen Barfield must have introduced Lewis to the subject but it remained a source of regret to him that Lewis did not give it more attention. In his South Indian ashram he would nurture the feeling that if his friend had lived longer he might have gone on to study Hinduism in depth and perhaps have become a little less fundamentalist in the process. One weakness in Indian thought Dom Bede himself identified from the very first: in its emphasis on the one supreme reality it had tended to negate the reality of the finite world, but then was not this precisely the corrective needed in a society in which modern science had come to look upon the material world as the sole reality?

It was during the 1940s that meditation began to enter into his life. Each day after vespers the monks at Prinknash had half an hour of meditation, but it was meditation of a kind that Dom Bede would regard with hindsight as slightly unsystematic: 'You just let your thoughts go.' Concurrent with his reading of eastern philosophy, he began to use the Jesus prayer – 'Lord Jesus, Son of God, have mercy on me' – a prayer which he found very helpful when his mind began to wander and one which he has continued to use ever since. With time there would come a point where it seemed to him to be constantly present in his body. Whenever he sat to meditate it would start as if without prompting. On one or two occasions he would give it up for a while simply because it had begun to feel mechanical and Father Bede, ever somewhat wary of techniques, was reluctant to become too tied to any particular one, but he was not entirely sure that it really was a technique. To him it was more like a form of natural rhythm. Now he uses the Jesus prayer but if it changes and other words come he lets it change in an endeavour always 'to be open to the Spirit'.

It was during the 1940s also that brothers belonging to the French Congregation that had for many years occupied the Abbey at Farnborough, without permission to recruit vocations in England, found themselves unable to maintain it. They appealed to the Subiaco Congregation of which Prinknash was a member and to the Benedictines to take it over, and eventually the community at Prinknash agreed to do so, despite the fact that it had just assumed responsibility for the derelict ruins of Pluscarden Priory in Scotland. Pluscarden would not be fit for habitation for some time yet and Farnborough, having been originally erected as a memorial, was understood to carry a substantial endowment.

In the Spring of 1947 the Abbot of Prinknash sent what Abbot Dyfrig would later describe as 'a very good nucleus, the cream of the community' to St Michael's Abbey, Farnborough. Among these twenty-five monks was Father Bede Griffiths who was installed as their Superior on 29 April 1947. His appointment as prior was not one which would have been generally anticipated at that stage, despite the fact that he had been recognized from the first as both a natural leader and a man of prayer. He had also made the perfect guestmaster gifted with that rare ability to be there when he was wanted and not when he was not. Most of the community saw him as a future abbot of Prinknash, but it was early days yet. What seems to have clinched the decision was one of those unexpected twists of circumstance that so frequently afterwards appear providential. Shortly prior to the acquisition of Farnborough, the Abbot of Prinknash was due to give a lecture in Glasgow but at the last minute found himself unable to go because of a severe attack of gout. In his place he sent Dom Bede who made such a tremendous success of the occasion that the tide of approbation lingered with him long afterwards.

Dom Bede himself was pleased by his installation as prior but embarrassed by the authority and the respect that it brought with it. It is possible that he also foresaw some of the difficulties his new position would entail. In a letter of congratulations dated simply 'April 15' in which the year remains unspecified but which may well refer to Father Bede's appointment as prior, C.S. Lewis made mention of his friend's anticipation of a cross:

My dear Dom Bede – I offer you my congratulations on your new office: my prayers you know you already have. There will certainly, as you anticipate, be a cross somewhere in it, but one mustn't assume crosses any more than consolations. You remember in the *Imitation* 'the devil does not mind in the least whether he snares us by true or by false pictures of the future.' In my experience the cross seldom comes where it is anticipated.

There were certainly very tangible difficulties connected with the initiation of the foundation at Farnborough. The endowment attached to the Abbey proved to be insufficient even to pay the fuel bills. Prinknash found itself financing both Pluscarden and Farnborough, a position which very nearly brought disaster to all three. The pressure was on the community at Farnborough to make the beautiful baroque church, the farm and the estate financially independent. In the event, however, it was the fact that the Farnborough foundation was run a little too independently that, in Father Bede's view, brought his period as prior to an end. Despite the distance between the two foundations the monks at Farnborough were expected to work in consultation with Prinknash. Yet they were trying to run a farm. It was not always possible when he was called out in the middle of the night, possibly to a cow calving, to take directions first from Prinknash. It was this kind of consideration, the fact that he was seen to be going a little too much his own way which, according to Father Bede, gave rise to the tensions that would eventually, in 1952, induce the Abbot to transfer the Prior of Farnborough to Pluscarden, and no longer as prior. Abbot Dyfrig Rushton, though prepared to concede that Father Bede might at that time have been seen to be a little anxious to make Farnborough independent, offers a different version of events. Such considerations did not enter into the decision. In any case ultimate independence of the Mother house is the objective of all new foundations. There was nothing wrong with Father Bede striving for that. What was of greater concern was the fact that the finances at Farnborough were not going too well and it was felt that Father Bede was not quite the man to handle problems of that particular nature: 'I always think of Chesterton's remark – "When you're in trouble you don't want an efficient man, you want a genius." ' He was not sent to Pluscarden as prior because the foundation in Scotland already had a superior.

One thing is certain: there was more of a cross in Father Bede's removal to Pluscarden than he himself is prepared to acknowledge or perhaps even, after the passage of so many years, is able to recall. Now he remembers happiness at Farnborough and happiness at Pluscarden, tempered with perhaps a little disappointment and the recognition of the need not to cling to power but to let go of it with good grace. At the time a close friend received a letter from him expressing his anger and hurt in a way which was for Father Bede unprecedented.

Pluscarden was sited in a remote and unspoilt setting of great natural beauty. In a way it was exactly the sort of place to which he and Hugh and Martyn would have chosen to resort from Eastington. Yet a question mark hovers over whether Father Bede was quite so contented there as might perhaps have been anticipated. Nevertheless his years in Scotland were productive ones. During those years he became both Master of Studies and Novice Master in a way which won him the admiration of his fellow monks. As Novice Master he had only two novices in his charge and so had the time and the freedom in which to indulge his passion for Henry James, a choice which with detachment he would later regard as rather interesting because of the characteristics he felt he shared with James – 'terribly intellectual yet getting into the emotional and the very subtle psychological world, observing the whole emotional world, in a way entering it and yet keeping away from it'. He was also free to write himself. He wrote articles, upon which C.S. Lewis would comment in his letters, and it was while he was at Pluscarden that he wrote *The Golden String*, a remarkable autobiography and testament to his spiritual journey thus far. It was written at the suggestion of Richard Rumbold, a writer and a friend from Oxford days, who as a Catholic homosexual felt himself rejected by the Church. Father Bede acknowledges that he might now find it difficult to write about himself but at the time he found it relatively easy to write with some degree of objectivity about experiences that had occurred some twenty years previously. He wrote then as he would invariably write thereafter and as he talks, with exceptional lucidity and without correction. Inevitably with so literary a background he has always wanted to write well but he finds that when the time is right his writing comes as if from a source outside himself and he is able to look upon his books and articles as if they were the works of someone else.

During his period as Prior of Farnborough Father Bede had come into contact with an Indian whose lifelong desire it had been to introduce the monastic life into the Church in India. Father Benedict Alapatt had been professed as a monk in a European monastery but his proposition was that a Benedictine foundation should be started in India from Prinknash. Not surprisingly, Father Bede had taken more than a passing interest in the proposal and the then Abbot had given it his support, but the plan had eventually been stopped by the Holy See because there was already a Benedictine House in existence not far from the location Father Alapatt had suggested. By 1955, however, the possibility of a foundation in India had again presented itself. This time the idea was together with Father Benedict Alapatt to start a foundation in Kengeri independently, not from Prinknash. For this Father Bede would need to obtain an indult of exclaustration after which he would be answerable, not to the Abbot at Prinknash but to the bishop in India. Indian philosophy had continued to preoccupy him during his time in Scotland. Time and time again the subject recurs in his correspondence with Lewis, and his other writings bear witness to the importance he already attributed to Hinduism: 'Certainly from a Christian point of view', wrote Father Bede in one of the concluding chapters of *The Golden String*, 'the importance of Indian philosophy can hardly be over-estimated. It marks the supreme achievement of the human mind in the natural quest of a true conception of God.' After some years of studying Vedanta he had begun to perceive in it something lacking in the western world and in the western Church. People in the West were living from one half of their soul, from the conscious, rational level and they needed to discover the other half, the unconscious, intuitive dimension. Aware that this was true of his own existence, he wanted to experience in his own life the marriage of these two dimensions: the rational and the intuitive, the conscious and the unconscious, the masculine and the feminine. Already he was beginning to seek, although possibly at that time he would not have been able to define it in quite those terms, the 'marriage of East and West'. Then, he wrote to a friend, 'I want to discover the other half of my soul.'

A priest who met Father Bede at that time recalls him remarking upon his deep desire to go to India and see for himself the religious life there and wondering however he would get there. In the chill of Scotland the pull of the southern sun reinforced the call for one who had always hated the cold, and so from Pluscarden he wrote to the Abbot requesting permission to go to India on this new basis. The Abbot's response was that there was too much of Father Bede's own will in what he asked, and Father Bede, doubtless not without a struggle, found himself able to say that if it was the Abbot's will he would go, but that otherwise he would not press the matter. 'The surrender of the ego', he would reflect in his old age, 'is the only way in life.' It was some time later, after Father Bede had abandoned all expectations of seeing for himself the India to which he felt so strongly drawn, that the Abbot wrote to him suggesting that he should go.

Even then the way was not clear of all obstacles. Exclaustration presented no undue difficulties, but just before he and Father Alapatt were due to set sail, a telegram arrived from India telling him not to come. It was only after being advised to ignore the instruction that he and Father Alapatt boarded the ship that would take them on their three-week journey from the Port of London via the Straits of Gibraltar, Suez and Aden to Bombay. The monastic life in England and Scotland had taught him many things, not least of them the true meaning and spirit of obedience and self-sacrifice. It had done much to temper and mature the over-eager young man of Eastington. 'Praised be St Benedict and his life of prayer and obedience', Hugh Waterman would write of his friend in March 1980 with the licence born of many years of affection, 'he is much more now a pervasive light than a consuming flame.'

Walter Griffiths,
Alan Griffiths' father

Alan with his mother,
Harriet Lilian Griffiths

Alan Griffiths c.1926

Alan (standing, second from left) in the rugby team at Christ's Hospital, 1923

Father Bede with Father Benedict Alapatt shortly before leaving for India in 1955

*With Martyn Skinner
during a visit to England
in 1959*

*The meditation hall,
Saccidananda Ashram*

The temple
Saccidananda Ashram

Father Bede's hut

The library
Saccidananda Ashram

*With the Prior General of
the Camaldoli Order
on the banks of
the River Cauvery*

*With the
President of India,
1986*

Amaldas

The brothers

Cristudas

Bede Griffiths

8

A Marriage of East and West

The slow journey to India by boat and his first direct experience of the East at Port Said and Aden evoked in Father Bede an immediate fascination with what he saw as a world of immeasurable beauty and vitality. His first impressions were very different from my own which had been shaped and perhaps distorted by an encounter on the bus ride from Delhi airport with an emaciated woman, who thrust her tiny baby through the window to beg as we halted at a congested junction. Tired as I was after a sleepless flight, her gaunt and prematurely wrinkled face, the hope and then the anger and dejection as the bus pulled away before I had had time to register precisely what it was she wanted, had left a powerful impression, and those desperate features had seemed to me then the face of all India. In the swarming mass of humanity that closed upon him in Bombay, Father Bede saw not so much the poverty and the misery but the grace and the beauty of the human form. I had gone to India, albeit with inexpressible yearnings, prepared to meet a wonderful people, but wonderful in its emphasis on the spiritual rather than the material, in its unaccountably joyful transcendence of poverty and wretchedness. Father Bede had gone there to discover the 'other half of his soul'. What we shared was possibly a tendency to make of what we saw the vehicle for our preconceived perceptions: inevitably we both saw first what we had gone there to seek.

In India Father Bede was struck by beauty but not so much now by the beauty of nature as by the beauty of human nature, by what Blake had called the 'human form divine'. Seeing for the first time the colour of Indian clothes, the grace and spontaneity of movement of the Indian people, he felt himself to be in the presence of a hidden power of nature. These women in brightly coloured saris, the men often naked to the waist, the children laughing and playing in their nudity were living from the 'unconscious'. People in the West, dominated by the conscious mind, went about their business, each trapped in his ego, and the rigid determination of their minds was reflected in their stiff awkward movements and their often drab clothes. In the East people lived not from the conscious mind but from the unconscious, from the body not from the mind. This was the secret of their abundance of life and joy, of a natural spontaneous beauty which they shared with flowers and animals. Yet theirs was not merely animal life and beauty for it had the grace of human intelligence. They lived from the unconscious, but it was the human unconscious, from what Jung had termed the anima as opposed to the animus.

Given that every human being was both masculine and feminine, in a man the masculine aspect or animus was usually dominant, and in the woman the feminine or anima. In every person a certain balance or harmony must be achieved and the same was true of the world as a whole. The man who had grown up in an environment which had suggested to him that in a sense those about him had no sex was now conscious of the interplay of the masculine and the feminine in the most profound and comprehensive way. In the East, as Father Bede saw it, the feminine aspect, the intuitive, passive, sympathetic power of the mind was dominant, while in the West the masculine aspect, the rational, active, aggressive power of the mind prevailed. In time he would come to express the view that the future of the world depended on the 'marriage' of these two minds, the conscious and the unconscious, the rational and the intuitive, the active and the passive. In time he would also find it possible to conceive of a development of science and technology which would seek not to dominate nature after the fashion of the West but to work in harmony with it, building upon the basis of a village economy as Mahatma Gandhi had sought to do, and so creating a new culture in which man and nature, and reason and intuition would be brought into harmony. From the first, however, India highlighted another dimension to his longstanding rejection of the industrialism and 'uglification' of modern western civilization. It was the product of the aggressive, rational mind of the West.

It was not in this respect alone that India would make a powerful impression on him. The 'golden string' which had been offered to him that summer's evening at school had led him to the discovery of God, of Christ and of the Church. India was a land which readily understood and accepted experiences such as he had undergone when he had felt himself in some way to 'go beyond' the realms of thought and senses and imagination. India was a land of the imagination. It was naturally religious and naturally contemplative. It was also a place where it had always been understood that there was a higher mode of knowledge than sense or reason – the knowledge of spiritual intuition, a knowledge not dependent on the senses or on any logical process, but on the soul's direct, intuitive awareness of itself. India would nurture that side of Father Bede which craved a less discursive, less rational understanding, or rather experience, of God. By the time he left England to embark upon a physical journey he had thought that his journey of another kind was nearer to its end, but in India he would discover that he must retrace that path to make new discoveries about God, about Christ and about the Church. The period of his life which began in India was less capable of being made subject to concise definition. There he was to discover the limitations of what he had thought he had known so clearly, and it is perhaps not insignificant that he would find it difficult to look upon the second half of his life in the same carefully structured manner as he had reviewed the first in *The Golden String*.

From his first days in Bombay he was aware that it was something more than the conscious and unconscious search for harmony between man and nature that so attracted him to the Indian culture. What seemed to meet a very profound need in him was the consciousness of a power beyond both man and nature which penetrated everything and was the real source of the beauty and vitality of Indian life. Over twenty-five years after he first set foot upon Indian soil, Father Bede would write in *The Marriage of East and West* of an early experience that had brought this message home to him most clearly. He had visited the Cave of Elephanta outside Bombay and there through a forest of pillars that created an atmosphere of mystery and immensity he had approached the great figure of Shiva Maheswara – the Great God – with his three faces, representing his benign and terrible and contemplative aspects. From a recess in the wall it loomed out of the darkness. 'It is colossal and overwhelming at first,' Father Bede would explain, 'but when you look into the front face you see that it is in deep contemplation. There is absolute peace there, infinitely distant yet infinitely near, solemn, benign, gentle and majestic. Here carved in stone is the very genius of India and the East.' This was what he had come to India to find, the contemplative dimension of human existence, which the West had almost lost and the East was in danger of losing. To stand before the figure of Shiva Maheswara in the Cave of Elephanta was to encounter that hidden depth of existence, 'springing from the depth of nature and the unconscious, penetrating all human existence and going beyond into the mystery of the infinite and eternal, not as something remote and inaccessible, but as something almost tangible engraved in this stone'. This was the secret he had come to discover. 'The mind of the East is open not only to man and nature in an intuitive understanding, but also to that hidden Power which pervades both man and nature and reveals to those who are attuned to it the real meaning of human existence.'

After more than thirty years in India Father Bede would acknowledge that he had been 'very favoured' when he first arrived there. He had stayed only in attractive places and it had taken him many years really to see the negative aspects of Indian life which even then would not dispel his feeling of love and sympathy. From the first he experienced a sense of oneness with the Indian people that was 'almost physical' and although it would be a very long time before he felt that he was even beginning to understand their psychology he sensed at once that amongst them he would find the side of life which had been lacking from his earlier years and from his middle class British family. The Indian family was to him 'one of the most beautiful things in the world'. The Indian village was made up of families held together in the closest bonds of affection. Indian children slept in the same room as their parents, they saw the animals copulating and grew naturally at ease with their own sexuality. Village life though materially poor, was full of beauty and the people lived very close to nature. Father Bede had long held the view that the spirit of the Christian life was normal in a village. In large cities life became dehumanized to some extent. Indeed, when the inhabitants exceeded a certain number such dehumanization was almost inevitable and so Father Bede's vision of an ideal town was Thomas Hardy's idea of a town in which a butterfly could fly in one end and out the other. In India something in the region of 80 per cent of the population lived in villages. It was in one of these, the village of Kengeri near Bangalore, that Father Bede and Father Alapatt first bought a property and began their monastic life together. The intention since Father Alapatt had first brought his suggestion to the monks at Prinknash had been to start a Benedictine foundation and, fresh to India as he was, Father Bede thought then that the normal Benedictine life in the Latin rite, as it had come down in the Middle Ages in Europe, was all that would be required. Though he was deeply committed to the continued study of Indian thought, the idea of changing his style of life had not as yet occurred to him. The occupants of the modern bungalow in Kengeri wore the traditional Benedictine habit with shoes and socks. They built a chapel in western style and they took their meals sitting at a table, eating with spoons, knives and forks. Their cells were simply furnished with wooden beds and straw mattresses, a table, a chair and a shelf for clothes and books. It was not that Father Bede had not recognized the particular importance of a life of poverty and simplicity in the Indian context. In fact, Lewis, with characteristic discernment had written to him early in 1954 of what he considered would be the necessary approach to the Indian people:

> I suspect that a great going-to-meet-them is needed not only on the level of thought but in method. A man who had lived all his life in India said, 'That country might be Christian now if there had been *no* Missions in our sense but many single missionaries walking the roads with their begging bowls. For that is the sort of Holy Man India believes in and she will never believe in any other.'

It was not long, however, before Father Bede discovered that what he considered simplicity constituted for the residents of the local village hitherto unheard of luxury.

Contact with the people in and around Bangalore was not only to show Father Bede a new standard of poverty and simplicity, it was also to enable him to see something of living Hinduism. The fact that the villagers were poor did not mean that they were not cultured. There was an old man in Kengeri who was a Sanskrit scholar, and from him Father Bede learned much of traditional Hindu wisdom. There were also several university students, well acquainted with western ways, who soon became regular visitors to the bungalow. When they discovered that it contained many books on Indian life and philosophy, they befriended the two Benedictine monks and invited them into their homes. One of these students became a particularly close friend of Father Bede. He was a great admirer of western culture and in many respects western in his own thinking, but he seemed to experience no sense of incongruity when he sat on the floor to eat his meals with his hand or when he made his weekly visits to the temple of the monkey god Hanuman sited not far from the monastery to conduct the worship there. His friendship brought home to Father Bede the way in which a primeval religion and culture could exist side by side with western ways. At this time Father Bede was studying Sanskrit with Raimundo Panikkar whose mother was a Spanish Catholic and whose father came from a well-known Hindu family and who embodied in a unique way the meeting of East and West.

He had been brought up in Europe, had taken degrees in science, philosophy and theology, and had returned to India to discover his Indian heritage. Together the two men explored the temples of the old Mysore State and found there architecture and sculpture of a beauty and refinement equal to the finest Gothic art and together they came to an appreciation of the deep hidden meaning beyond the outward form of beauty.

Touring the temples of Mysore and later of Tamil Nadu, Father Bede did not fail to discover how the whole Hindu temple was a shrine to the inner Spirit, the Atman, which to the Hindu is the ground of all existence. He was led through the outer walls decorated with figures of animals and men and gods, and so by stages through the different levels of life in this world to the *garbha griha*, the 'cave of the heart' where there was often nothing but a lingam, the bare stone representing the formless divinity, the absolute godhead which was beyond all 'name and form'. The sexual origin of the lingam did not, of course, elude him, but to him it served to emphasize the profundity of understanding in ancient India. Sex then was regarded as something 'holy' and still was in modern India, in Father Bede's view, except where the Indian spirit had been corrupted by the West. The lingam was a natural symbol of the sacred 'source of life' which was seen not as a mere biological reality but as the absolute Being, the eternal reality which was life and consciousness and bliss – the infinite, formless *saccidananda*. Sitting down one day beside a shrine on a riverbank, he found in it nothing but a roughly-carved lingam and yoni, the male and female organs. To him they seemed a touching expression of the sense of the 'sacred', the awareness of the essential holiness of nature and of faith in her generative powers.

The sense of the sacred as something pervading the whole order of nature was possibly the deepest impression left on Father Bede by his early experiences of Indian life and it was one which would remain with him throughout the years that followed. In India, he discovered, the earth was sacred. So it was that no ploughing or sowing or harvesting could take place without some religious rite. Eating was a sacred action and every meal was looked upon as a sacrifice to God. Water was sacred and so no devout Hindu would take a bath without invoking the sacred power of it. Air was sacred, the breath of life which came from God and sustained all living creatures. Fire was sacred especially in its source, the sun which brought life and light to all created things. Plants and trees were sacred, especially certain ones such as the banyan. So too were animals, especially the cow which gave her milk as a mother. Finally, every man was sacred as a manifestation of God but especially a holy man, in whom the divine presence was more clearly visible. Father Bede was conscious that the sense of the sacred could lead to a kind of pantheism. It was for that very reason, he felt, that Christians were often on their guard against it, but though he believed that there was a form of pantheism in India, he was also certain that the ancient tradition of the *Vedas*, the *Upanishads* and the *Bhagavad Gita* was not pantheistic. Theirs was a vision of the *totally* immanent and the *totally* transcendent. That, he would later maintain, was the reality of the sacred – that the one divine mystery was manifested in the earth, in the water, and that was a profoundly Christian idea, the biblical idea that man was in the image of God. Yet the other side of the same idea, that the universe itself was sacred and mirrored God, was much less common in the West.

On one occasion, while he was in Bangalore, as he was coming away from the temple to Hanuman sited not far from the monastery Father Bede encountered an elderly Brahmin who spoke good English and had been educated in a Christian school. Doubtless wondering what a Christian monk would make of a monkey-god, he explained to the stranger that God was manifested in every form in the universe, be it in plant or animal or man. Above all, however, he stressed that God was present in the human heart, and he proceeded to quote some stanzas of the *Bhagavad Gita* in the rhythmical chant which is used in the recitation of Sanskrit. To his eager listener this was a wonderful illustration of the sense of the sacred and an example of the deep roots of Hindu tradition, the sense of the one eternal spirit pervading the universe and manifested in all things, which had been enshrined in the doctrine of the *Upanishads* and the *Bhagavad Gita*, and come down into the life of the contemporary villager. Was it not precisely this sense of the sacred which the western world needed so urgently to recover? 'In the West,' Father Bede would write some years later in *Christian Ashram*, 'everything has become "profane"; it has been deliberately emptied of all religious meaning.' In medieval Europe the economic, social and political orders had been seen as subordinate to the spiritual order, to the life of prayer and communion with God, and a hierarchy had thus been established in which the life of everyone from the serf to the feudal lord could find its place. In part the ensuing process of 'profanation' was an inevitable reaction to the 'sacred order' of the Middle Ages, by which people were driven to concentrate more and more on secular and human values to the exclusion of religion. 'Yet now that the economic and social and political orders have won their independence', asserted Father Bede, 'they need to recover a religious basis if human life is not to be emptied of all ultimate meaning.'

Ancient India had experienced a social structure not dissimilar to that of medieval Europe. Ancient Indian society had been divided into four 'classes' as distinct from the multitude of castes that would afterwards develop. These classes consisted of the workers (*Sudras*) at the basis, then the farmers and merchants (*Vaisyas*), then the warriors or rulers (*Kshetryas*), and finally at the top the Brahmins or priests. Thus as in medieval Europe the priest who was concerned with man's relation to God, the ultimate reality, was placed at the head of the social order, so that all human life and culture was integrated with religion. In India this was reinforced by the four *ashramas* or stages of life through which a man was expected to pass. The first was that of the *brahmachari*, the student or 'seeker after God' who studied the Vedas, the 'eternal law', in which it was believed the source of all wisdom was to be found. Next there was the stage of the householder, during which a man married, raised a family, and prepared for the time when, having fulfilled his duty to society, he was expected to retire to the forest to meditate and make ready his soul for its release from this world. Finally, in the last stage, as a wandering *sannyasi*, he renounced the world altogether to give himself to God alone. It was probable that this had always been a more or less ideal scheme of life, but in contemporary India, Father Bede could still discern the profound understanding of the ultimate values of life which underlay such a scheme and which had been at the roots of the ancient social order in a way that he could not discern them in the contemporary western world. It was not that he was blind to what the West could offer the East but the advantages of advanced science and technology were already universally recognized. What he identified as the great gift of the East, the 'sense of the sacred' was less so. Yet it was a gift which should be welcomed not only by the western world in general but also by the Christian Church. If the West as a whole needed to relearn from the East the sense of a transcendent mystery which was immanent in everything and which gave an ultimate meaning to life, it was also clearly apparent to Father Bede that Hinduism had much to offer that could serve as inspiration to the Christian Church which had become so very largely a western religion.

Thinking along these lines had already been germinating in him before he left England. Today it does not seem perhaps so strikingly novel to suggest that the West and Christianity could learn from the East and from Hinduism. Quite how radical such thought was in the England of the 1950s is well illustrated by the fact that shortly before his departure from England Father Bede was invited by a friend from his Oxford days to have lunch in the House of Lords. When Father Bede suggested that Father Alapatt should join them for the occasion, the invitation was quietly dropped. In those days it was simply not acceptable to receive an Indian, even an Indian Christian priest, as a guest in the House of Lords. Yet in India Father Bede found himself not alone in his thinking. India represented for him a great expansion of his life in more than one sense. After the relative seclusion of the Benedictine life in England in India he began to travel more and in 1956 his travels brought him to Shantivanam, the Abode of Peace, and the ashram which Jules Monchanin and Henri Le Saux had founded six years previously. He stayed for a few days in one of three little huts set in a beautiful wilderness of palmyra trees where barely a track ran through the forest of thorns, and he found the attempt to harmonize Christian monastic tradition with Indian ascetic traditions fascinating and impressive.

Thereafter he would meet Father Monchanin in particular on a number of occasions. Not very long after Father Bede's arrival in India there was a meeting held in Bangalore by the Union for the Study of the Great Religions, an organization started by Radhakrishnan. It was a meeting on the scriptures of the great religions attended by representatives of all the religions in India including all the sects of Hinduism, at which both Father Bede and Father Monchanin were invited to give talks. Again, in 1957 a meeting was held in Madras on the saints of the great religions. There Father Bede spoke on the subject of St Benedict and Father Monchanin on St John of the Cross. Then, in the same year, a Catholic meeting was held on the theme of 'The Indian culture and the fullness of Christ'. The attempt really to discover a cultural structure for Christianity in India was one which Father Bede considered vital. At the meeting Father Monchanin made a very important speech. Sadly, there were many obstacles for him. He had a very strong French accent which made it difficult for people in general to follow his very profound thinking. Yet he was in his element when speaking in French to a small group of scholars. Father Bede responded to his intelligence and identified in him a very holy and a very humble man for whom Saccidananda Ashram was in many ways a Calvary and to whom, in later life he would recognize, he owed a great deal. In the year of Monchanin's death Father Bede once more visited Shantivanam for what was one of the highpoints in the history of the ashram. It was an occasion for dialogue between Hindus and Christians which gave the two French Fathers a glimpse of what they had been hoping for, a gathering attended by the Brahmins and others from Kulitalai at which, thanks to the presence of a Rumanian Catholic who had been a member of the Ramakrishna order and who was well versed in Hindu ritual, a service was held incorporating many elements of Hindu worship.

Father Bede was never quite as close to Henri Le Saux despite the latter's indisputable warmth and affectionate nature but after Monchanin's death the friendship with the co-founder of Saccidananda Ashram continued. Abhishiktananda was the organizer, together with Dr Cuttat, the Swiss Ambassador in New Delhi, of a succession of meetings in the north of India at which Christians of a variety of denominations came together to read the Bible and the *Upanishads* side by side. Initially, at least, no Hindus were invited. Rather it was an attempt on the part of Christians to open themselves to the Hindu tradition, an attempt which was not particularly successful but in which Father Bede was pleased to take part. Already he had recognized that people were conscious now, as never before, that they belonged to 'one' world. Politically and economically no one nation could stand apart from the rest. He was convinced that the different religions of the world also could no longer exist apart as they had done in the past, each forming a separate cultural unit; that it was only when a meeting of religions had taken place that an adequate spirituality would be found to meet the needs and the challenges of the modern world; and that in this meeting India with its spiritual tradition second to none in the history of mankind would have a decisive part to play.

After two years at Kengeri it became apparent to Father Bede and Father Alapatt that it would not be possible to make a permanent foundation in Bangalore. Those two years of direct experience of Hinduism and of the Christian Church in India had served to endorse the view which Father Bede shared with Monchanin and Le Saux that if a genuine meeting of East and West was to take place it must be at the deepest level of their experience and that this could best be brought about through the monastic life. He was convinced that if the monastic life could be introduced into India, it would be something profoundly congenial to the Indian mind. The ascetic tradition with its centre in the ashram was, he recognized, one of the most basic institutions of Indian life – Buddhist, Jain and Hindu. In modern times also there had been a great revival of this ascetic tradition: not only had the great mystics such as Sri Aurobindo and Ramana Maharshi centred their lives on the ashram but a great reformer like Mahatma Gandhi, who had long held a special attraction for Father Bede, had been led spontaneously to base his life on an ashram. Through the influence of the Ramakrishna Order, which Vivekananda founded to continue the work of his master, social work had been introduced as an integral element of Hindu monastic life, a fact which had brought it much closer to Christian monasticism. The aim of the monastic life remained always the 'search for God' or for 'liberation' in Hindu terms, but under the influence of Gandhi and Vivekananda the search for God had come to be intimately concerned with care for one's fellow-men. So it was that Christian monasticism was conceived by St Benedict with its basic motive of seeking God in a life of prayer and asceticism, but with its custom of manual work and hospitality which brought the monks into vital contact with the contemporary world, could be seen to have a natural affinity with the ascetic life which Father Bede had found already to exist in India.

There was a necessary separation from the world in a monastic life, a discipline of silence and solitude which was required for the discovery of the inner centre of a monk's being, but this separation need not necessarily, as Father Bede had himself come to feel at Prinknash, cut a monk off from the world. On the contrary it could enable him to meet the world at the deepest level of its being. One of the sayings of the monastic fathers was that 'A monk is one who separates himself from all men in order that he may be united with all men.' It was at this point that Father Bede felt that the meeting of religions must ultimately take place, for here all were one in the Christ who had said 'in as much as you do it to the least of these my brethren you do it to me'. It was at this point also that the life of a monk was integrated with the life of the world, for to meet another individual in Christ was necessarily to be concerned with his whole being, not only his soul but his body also. In India, surrounded as he was by people who were living at the barest level of subsistence and who were constantly in danger of falling below it, it was almost impossible for him not to be concerned with the problem of poverty, that of an appropriate poverty in his own life and that of an intolerable poverty in the lives of many amongst whom he lived. The need for raising the standard of living was irrefutable, but at the same time, like Mother Teresa and so many others who worked amongst the poorest of the poor, he had recognized that those who in the material sense had nothing were often possessed of spiritual riches: a capacity for patient and cheerful endurance, a spirit of sharing, of co-operation and of love. An Indian friend, in response to Father Bede's question as to what the real religion of the occupants of one particularly poor village was, once remarked 'Oh, their religion is love.' So often economic and social advancement brought with it the undermining of religious faith, the rupture of relationships and the disintegration of village life. If material progress was to bring real and enduring happiness, Father Bede was convinced that it must be integrated with the spiritual life of the people. Their social, moral and religious life must be developed along with their economic condition and their general education.

The move from Bangalore was made against the backcloth of thinking of this kind and in the realization that if he wished to approach the level of life not merely of the *sannyasi* in India, but even of the ordinary villager, a drastic change would have to take place in his mode of living. Near the tamarind tree at Shantivanam stood a hut constructed by Father Francis Mahieu, a Cistercian of the abbey of Scourmont in Belgium. He too had arrived in India in 1955. He had come in search of the contemplative life in Indian form and for a year had lived at Saccidananda Ashram, but by 1958 he felt called to start a new foundation along slightly different lines. Father Francis held the view that if the contemplative life was really to take root in India it must first be planted where the Catholic life was already at its strongest. Together he and Fathers Bede and Alapatt therefore moved to Kerala, the most Christian state in India, the very heart of the Indian Catholic Church, with the intention of establishing what, if the bungalow at Kengeri had been a monastery, would be a monastic ashram, a foundation which was very strongly in the monastic tradition but one that was imbued with a more Indian character.

9

Kurisumala Ashram

Kerala is a narrow strip of land on the southwest coast of India which extends some 360 miles from north to south while its breadth is a mere twenty miles at its narrowest point. Inland from its densely populated coastal lowlands are high mountain ranges dominated by an impressive peak called *Aneimudi* or 'Elephant forehead'. At 8,840 feet it is the highest peak in India south of the Himalayas. Nearby *Kurisumala* (Mountain of the Cross) has a more modest elevation of 4,000 feet but it is a very rugged mountain capped with bare rock alleviated only by patches of grass and shrubs hiding in the folds of crags, precipitous ridges and wooded gulleys. To the south it overlooks the fertile coconut and pepper gardens once the property of the Poonjar rajahs but from this side it is virtually inaccessible. At the end of the nineteenth century the mountain caught the imagination of a group of intrepid and devout men who placed a cross on the summit and later erected a small shrine. Since that time it has been held as a holy place attracting thousands of pilgrims each year at Eastertide. The pass giving access to Kurisumala is on the eastern slope while to the north and west it is bordered by a precipitous drop of more than 2,000 feet. It was on a hill adjacent to that mountain, in a wild and solitary place, not long previously the haunt of elephant and bison, that in 1958 the founders of Kurisumala Ashram were given eighty-eight acres of land.

The tiny community arrived in March and began at once the task of constructing a hut of bamboo and plaited palm leaves that would serve them as a shelter while plans for the building of the ashram proper were laid. It was only a matter of weeks before the monsoon came. In the downpour the floor of their fragile hut, which was made of earth, became so damp that its occupants had to cover it first with straw and then with planks in order to keep dry. In furious winds and unrelenting rain Father Bede and his companions struggled to put a tinned sheet roof on the as yet incomplete stone building only to find that one Sunday afternoon in July, with a terrifying noise, the whole roof, about 5,000 square feet of corrugated sheets, beams, purlins and rafters, was lifted into the air and folded in two like a portfolio. It was a disheartening experience but the damage was soon rectified and within a few months they moved into the new building with the roof now securely anchored to the ground.

Experience of struggling to combat the elements with the simplest of means also enabled them to draw nearer to the condition of the poor of India and of their neighbours, the few settlers who had ventured up from the plains to try and scratch their livelihood from the hill slopes. These settlers often gave up all idea of cultivation above 2,000 ft for the crops were poor and every year the soil was washed away by the torrential rains which could sometimes last from June right through to October. Those who remained turned to cattle keeping. They usually built a shed of jungle timber and grass in which they sheltered their cattle for the night. During the day the cows, which were often dry, roamed indiscriminately over the grasslands.

At Kurisumala Father Francis, Father Bede and their first two companions followed the tradition of Hindu *sannyasis* by wearing the *kavi* habit, by going barefoot, sitting on the floor, eating with their hands and sleeping on mats, but these were all traditional customs not only of *sannyasis* but also of normal life amongst India's poor; so too was the custom of making do with the minimum of furniture. Food at the ashram was according to Hindu tradition strictly vegetarian, consisting of rice and vegetables and fruit, with milk and *ghee*, or purified butter. The community recognized that poverty was an essential mark of 'holiness' in India. They also wished to identify themselves with the ordinary Indian villager.

In order to support themselves they set up a dairy farm. From early days in India ashrams had been associated with *goshalas* or cattle farms. An ancient Hindu tradition still alive in independent India regarded the *goshala* as a place where ageing cows were still cared for and where they could remain until their death. This view could still be traced in Mahatma Gandhi's *Ashram Observances in Action* which recommended *goseva*, or cow service. Gandhi, however, was also concerned with reconciling such service with economics. Well aware of the tremendous burden imposed on the nation by its cattle population, he recognized that the 250 million head of cattle, about half of which were useless, were really competing with the human population for the food the land could produce. He therefore advocated the improvement of breeds and the increase in quantity and the enriching of the quality of milk so that the cow could become less of a burden and more of a supporter of the country which nurtured her. It was this kind of *goseva* which Kurisumala Ashram endeavoured to pursue. In cooperation with the government the monks imported two Jersey bulls from England to be used in the insemination not only of their own cows but of all the cattle in the area. In return the government agreed to set up a 'key village centre' at Kurisumala with veterinary staff. This meant that the ashram could take its part in the great 'community development' plan for all India and at the same time receive the assistance of expert advice whenever it was needed. It also meant that without involving themselves in any external activity the community was able to enter fully into the life of the people in the locality, people who were mostly very poor.

It was not that there was not wealth in Kerala. In the plains there was an abundance of rice, and coconuts were grown and used for every conceivable purpose, providing food and fuel, oil for lamps, thatching for roofs and coir for matting and brushes. On the hills and lower mountain slopes there were large tea and coffee plantations, originally the work of Europeans but now mostly owned by Indians. This made it one of the richest states in India, but at the same time it was one of the most densely populated not only in India but in the world, a fact which inevitably posed a grave economic problem. Kerala also had the distinction of being the most literate and educated state in the Indian Union, and it was this combination of wealth and poverty, of education and high unemployment which Father Bede saw as accounting for the growth of communism in the area. His own vision of the ideal social and economic life was neither communist nor capitalist. In his view capitalism, by concentrating on the freedom of the individual led to a competitive form of society and to the exploitation of man and nature which bore within it the seeds of disintegration, however much it might be corrected by the aims of social justice. Communism, while endeavouring to correct the evils of capitalism, suppressed the freedom of the individual and led to forcible collectivization. For one who held ever before him the Christian ideal depicted in the Acts of the Apostles where the disciples were 'of one heart and soul, and none of them called any of his possessions his own, but they had all things in common', somewhere between capitalism and communism lay the ideal of Mahatma Gandhi and his spiritual son, Vinoba Bhave. Gandhi's vision of the salvation of India through her villages, through spinning and through agriculture, his mistrust of modern machinery as a remedy that would inevitably lead to unemployment on a vast scale, his lack of faith in the centralized bureaucratic state and in industrialism, his concern with the building of a non-violent order of society held an obvious attraction for Father Bede. In Vinoba's campaign, which went even further than Gandhi's in demanding 'non-possessiveness' and asking the Indian people willingly to renounce their right to private property, Father Bede identified something to which they might well respond as people who were naturally communally minded and inclined to share (hence the spontaneous appeal of some of the more positive aspects of communism in India). He also saw in it a call for the fulfilment of the gospel, for that renunciation of property which the early Christians made.

In his periodical *Harijan* (meaning literally 'children of

God', a name which the Mahatma gave to the untouchables)
Gandhi had written many years previously:

> Man's ultimate aim is the realization of God, and all his
> activities, social, political, religious, have to be guided by the
> ultimate aim of the vision of God. The immediate service of all
> human beings (*sarvodaya*) becomes a necessary part of the
> endeavour, simply because the only way to find God is to see
> him in his creation and to be one with it. This can only be done
> by the service of all (*sarvodaya*).

Sarvodaya, meaning 'service of all' was the name given by
Gandhi to the movement which he began towards a new life
in the villages of India and which Vinoba would afterwards
continue by walking from village to village, trying to induce
the rich to give land to the poor and attempting to awaken a
spirit of co-operation in the villages. It was also a movement
with a spiritual basis in accordance with the best traditions of
Hinduism. Gandhi's life work was based on the two
principles – truth (*satya*) and non-violence (*ahimsa*). By truth
he meant adherence to the inner principle of Being, the
Atman or Spirit, which governs the universe, and by non-
violence he meant far more than a negative ideal. Rather he
meant the basic respect for every man as an image of God, in
whom the universal Spirit dwells. The social and economic
reforms which the *Sarvodaya* movement sought to introduce
were seen essentially as a means for people to 'realize'
themselves as human beings, and this in Hindu thought
necessarily meant the realization of their fundamental
relation to God, the ground of all being. What was perhaps
new to Hinduism was the assertion that this could only come
about through the realization of the individual's relation to
his neighbour and to the land upon which he depended.
Gandhi and Vinoba had striven to abolish all distinction of
caste and seen the land as belonging to the people as a whole
to be worked on a basis of co-operation. Not surprisingly
Father Bede identified in such a view what was in a sense the
confirmation of what he had long felt: the happiness of man
could ultimately only be found when he found once more the
right relationship with God, with nature and with his fellow

men. It was also a meeting point between the Hindu and the Christian ideal.

Together with the manual work, the rearing of cattle and the cultivation of better vegetables and food crops, which the community at Kurisumala regarded simultaneously in the light of Gandhi's 'bread-labour' and in the context of the Rule of St Benedict which stated that 'then only are they truly monks when they live by the labour of their hands like our Fathers and the Apostles', the search for other meeting points went on. From its first arrival in Kerala the community had used the Syrian instead of the Latin rite in its worship. Father Francis Mahieu, who had come initially to Kerala to learn Sanskrit, had discovered that the majority of Christians there belonged to the Syrian Church and had begun to see the Syrian rite as one more firmly rooted in the Indian culture. The earliest historical evidence suggests that a Christian Church existed in India from at least the fourth century and that this Church formed part of the Persian or East Syrian Church. A fact which is frequently overlooked in relation to what has now become very largely a western religion is that Christianity, while it was spreading westwards through Asia Minor to Greece and Rome, was also spreading eastwards through Syria and Mesopotamia. The focal point of this Eastern Church was Edessa, a city on the borders of Syria and Mesopotamia, where the local people spoke a form of Aramaic, the language of Jesus and of his disciples, which later became known as Syriac. It was this Syrian Church which in time spread to India. In time also it became separated from the Churches of the West. The forces of Islam overwhelmed it to a substantial degree and today it survives only in small pockets in the Middle East. In Kerala, however, it had flourished more than any other Christian Church.

The discovery of the Syrian Church opened up to Father Bede a whole world of Eastern Christianity of which he had known little until then. Syrian Christianity demonstrated the possibility of an oriental form of the Christian faith, distinct from all its occidental forms. Greek and Latin Christianity were essentially western in their style and habit of thought, but the Syrian Church was essentially eastern. It belonged to the Middle East and bore everywhere on it the marks of its origins. It was in this form that Christianity seemed most naturally capable of adaptation to the peoples of the East. Yet the Syrian Church in itself did not provide the solution to all divisions, be they between Christian and Hindu or between Christian and fellow Christian. There were Syrian Catholics, Syrian Orthodox and Syrian Protestants and, to further complicate the issue, in the fifth century a division had taken place within the Syrian Church. At that juncture the East Syrians had adopted the Nestorian form of the Christian faith with its emphasis on the human nature of Christ and the West Syrians had adopted the Monophysite form with its emphasis on the divine nature in Christ. In Kerala the community was immediately confronted with these divisions when, not without creating a certain conflict, they chose to adopt the West Syrian Malankara rite. It had fewer representatives in Kerala but Father Francis had from the first been impressed by the fact that it used the vernacular. Furthermore it was a less Latinized and much purer form of the Syrian tradition.

Even the Syrian Church in its purest form, however, belonged really to the Middle East and was still very far from the culture of the Far East. At most, Father Bede felt, it could serve as a bridge by which Christianity could eventually be adapted to the culture of India, China and Japan. The task of the Church in the Far East must be to enter fully into the cultural inheritance of these peoples. The adoption of certain external customs and the use of the vernacular in the liturgy was only a first step. The great need as far as the Far East was concerned was, Father Bede recognized, to have a theology constructed on the basis of Indian and Chinese thought and a Christian spirituality which would draw on all the rich resources of eastern spirituality, Hindu, Buddhist, Taoist and Confucian. More particularly, in India what was needed was a Christian Vedanta and a Christian Yoga, a system of theology which made use not only of the terms and concepts but of the whole structure of thought of the Vedanta, in the same way that the Greek Fathers had used Plato and

Aristotle; and a spirituality which would make use not only of the practices of *Hatha* Yoga, by which most people understood Yoga, but of the great systems of *Karma*, *Bhakti* and *Jnana* Yoga, the way of works or action, of love or devotion, and of knowledge or wisdom, through which the spiritual genius of India had been manifested for centuries.

Father Francis was a Cistercian and so under his leadership Kurisumala Ashram was run along Cistercian lines with a strong emphasis on silence, a substantial part of the communication between the monks being effected by means of sign language, on community life and worship seven times a day and upon manual labour. The rule of the ashram was to refrain from using outside labour although some concessions were made with regard to certain aspects of the farm work. Consequently members of the community were sometimes engaged for six or seven hours a day in strenuous physical work. It was a rigorous life style in which Father Bede did his share of cultivation, clearing of scrubland, felling trees and carrying the wood on his head up the steep hillside slopes. The work took its toll as did the climate. Each year when the monsoon came Kurisumala was swathed in cloud. For three months it was almost impossible to see out of the window. The atmosphere was so damp that a stove had to be kept burning in the library to prevent the books from being ruined. At intervals the clouds would part, the sun would come out, members of the community would rush to hang the bedding out to dry and then the rain would start all over again. It was a process which Father Bede would with hindsight profess to have enjoyed whilst at the same time conceding that it was quite an ordeal. At Kurisumala he developed an ulcer which he would attribute in part to the highly spiced Indian diet, in part to other factors. The stomach which had always been a problem for him protested once more. Nonetheless Father Bede committed himself to a demanding course of intellectual labour. A regular course of study was, he felt, an essential part of their monastic life. The fear and suspicion with which the spiritual tradition of Hinduism was approached by many Christians was largely the product of ignorance. To his own study of that spiritual tradition he added the learning of Syriac. He and Father Francis had already spent six months learning the basics of the language and celebrating the Qurbana (the Eucharist) at a Syro-Malankaran monastery of the Order of the Imitation of Christ before they began the ashram. Now, doubtless stimulated by the vision of the Syrian rite as a step towards a more Indian form of Christianity, he embarked upon the study of Syriac in earnest.

Despite his early talent for French, his aptitude for Classics and a working knowledge of Sanskrit, Father Bede claims to be unable to learn Indian languages. Over the years he has made attempts at Malayalam, Tamil and others. He has learnt the alphabets and managed to construct sentences but when he has talked no one has understood him. Nor has he been able to understand what others have been saying, even when he knows the vocabulary used – 'It is all a question of hearing.' Not without some regret, in his old age he would abandon all efforts to speak Indian languages, but Syriac he mastered during those years at Kurisumala to such a degree that he was able to translate into English the Book of Common Prayer of the Syrian Church. It was a task which captured his enthusiasm not only because of the historical importance of the rites and prayers but also because of the great beauty of the language. In a letter written a year before Lewis' death, Father Bede tried to communicate something of the enthusiasm he felt for liturgy as a means by which the Church entered most deeply into the life of a people, took root in a country and began an authentic growth, but Lewis was unresponsive. He had once remarked to Father Bede that he did not like Church services at all and hymns least of all, and that he thought Christianity should be a matter of a group of men meeting together to talk and share with one another. Lewis had a total lack of concern about the Church as an institution and the externals of worship, 'a kind of wearisome, get-together affair', did not appeal to him at all. As might perhaps have been predicted, he wrote back to Father Bede congratulating him on having learnt yet another language but adding:

I hardly share one of the purposes for which you use it. I cannot take an interest in liturgiology. I see very well that someone ought to feel it. If religion includes cult and cult requires order, it is somebody's business to be concerned with it. But not, I feel, mine. Indeed for the laity I sometimes wonder if our interest in liturgiology is not really rather a snare. Some people talk as if it were itself the Christian faith.

There had been a time when Alan Griffiths was probably as little interested as his friend in liturgy but the concept of the Church as the mystical body of Christ had been a vital factor in the process by which he became a Catholic, and he had gone on to see the liturgy of the Church as the worship of the Mystical Body of Christ or Christ himself, as St Augustine said, praying in his members. The whole sacramental and mystical side of religion was something which Father Bede felt to be slightly lacking in his friend, and on the strength of his own experience of Indian religion he would later express the view that Lewis' understanding of the place of mystical experience in religious life would have grown if he had been able to make a deeper study of Hinduism. As it was, Lewis died before any such opportunity arose. The two men met for the last time a month before his death in 1963 and it was Lewis who reminded his companion then that they had been friends for nearly forty years. Looking back on those years Father Bede could not help but marvel at the faithfulness with which Lewis had answered his letters, at the patience, warmth and humility with which he had dealt consistently with his one-time student. There had been few things in his life, Father Bede acknowledged, more precious to him than that friend-ship. It had not perhaps been a relationship of great emotional intimacy. The death of his much loved wife is marked in Lewis' correspondence with a brief sentence presented almost as an aside: 'I forget whether you know that my wife died in July.' Yet the relationship had been a constant and greatly valued stimulus to Father Bede.

Significantly Lewis, for all his lack of in-depth study of Hinduism, did not die without having placed his finger on what might be considered to be one of the prime difficulties in establishing a positive relationship between Hinduism and Christianity: 'The difficulty of preaching Christ in India is that there is no difficulty. One is up against true Paganism – the best sort of it as well as the worst – hospitable to all gods, naturally "religious", ready to take any shape but able to retain none.' It was a difficulty which Father Bede fully recognized. Christianity in India was always in danger of simply being absorbed into Hinduism in much the same way that in the early centuries Christ was in danger of becoming one of the gods of the Roman Empire. In Hinduism there was one, absolute, infinite, eternal Being, the Brahman, which was manifested in all the different forms of nature and life. The object of life was to realize the absolute, indivisible unity of this one Being, not simply mentally but spiritually, so that an individual discovered in the depths of his being an identity with this one Absolute. When this identity became known all differences disappeared; the absolute, simple identity of all being was experienced in an ecstasy of pure bliss. This was *moksha* and in the Hindu view all religions were but different paths to this one goal. Through the ages there had been a succession of 'great souls', who had attained to this knowledge of the supreme identity and had been able to show the path of realization to others. Among such 'great souls' whom Hindus would not hesitate to call incarnations of God were not only Rama and Krishna, the heroes of the Hindu epics, but also the Buddha, Christ and Mohammed together with spiritual leaders of modern times such as Ramakrishna and Ramana Maharshi. The Hindu view was all-embracing and answered the problem of diversity of religion from a Hindu point of view to perfection. Yet Father Bede, whilst recognizing all that Hinduism had to offer and identifying many common inheritances of a primordial tradition, finding in Hinduism ideas of trinity, of incarnation, of salvation and grace, of sacrifice and sacrament, also maintained that real and essential differences should be respected. The Christian idea of Trinity and incarnation, for example, was profoundly different from the Hindu, and the real way forward did not lie in pretending that such differences did not exist.

It was such a viewpoint that Father Bede would put to Vinoba in a village not far from Agra where the leader of the *Sarvodaya* movement was encamped in the course of one of his long walks through the villages of India. Vinoba was sixty-three at the time and dressed in a loincloth, shawl and sandals together with a curiously incongruous American-style green cap. His austere features with a white goatee beard would linger long in the memory of Father Bede as would the fact that (as Lewis had also done some years previously) the Hindu suggested that his English visitor should not concern himself unduly with differences of faith. Vinoba urged that they should unite together in those common principles of 'spirituality' which belonged to almost all religion. Against this Father Bede argued that ultimately there could be only one religion for mankind but that this one religion could not be reached by ignoring the essential differences which existed. Rather an attempt should be made to understand such differences and reconciliation should be sought through mutual understanding and dialogue. The idea of an 'ecumenical' movement corresponding to that which was already taking place among Christians was one which was acceptable to Vinoba as it would doubtless have been to most Hindus. What he further acknowledged was that a Christian whilst respecting other religious traditions was bound to hold to certain principles which he regarded essential to his religion and that he could not be expected to join in common prayer with Hindus if it was against his conscience. Father Bede's decision to give full co-operation to the *Sarvodaya* movement was dependent upon their agreement that no one who worked with the movement should be called upon to compromise his faith in any way. What Father Bede was seeking was not syncretism, a mixing on the surface of the different religions, with their peculiar cultural and symbolic expression, but to go beyond this to the reality they sought to express.

10

A Meeting in Christ

After years of study and meditation Father Bede would reach the view that there was one original and eternal truth enshrined in all religious traditions, but that as soon as this original truth began to be expressed, even in a Buddha or a Jesus, it was entering into the temporal world and so became subject to distortion. Each tradition whilst it enshrined the original truth explicated it in a particular way with historical, cultural and linguistic limitations. So the way forward lay through the discernment of the inner truth within each tradition. At the same time, even in the 1980s Father Bede would maintain that there was something unique in each tradition and that each had therefore its own unique contribution to make to the whole. The divisions even though they might exist at the level of the exoteric rather than the esoteric of belief should not therefore be ignored but explored. The point to which Father Bede aspired at Kurisumala, the establishing of all the great religions in a positive relationship to one another was blocked primarily by what he saw as the conflict between the Semitic group of religions, Judaism, Islam and Christianity, on the one hand, and the oriental religions, especially Hinduism and Buddhism on the other. The Hindu view of the unity of all religions was won, he recognized, at a price no orthodox Christian, Muslim or Jew could admit, for it meant that there was ultimately no difference between God and man and nature. All distinctions disappeared in the one absolute Being. This meant that in the final analysis the world and time and history were unreal. Their appearance was an effect of *avidya* or ignorance and when known for what they were, they disappeared, as he would put it, quoting from Sankara, in *Christian Ashram*, 'like the form of a snake which has been mistakenly superimposed on a rope'. For their part the Jew, the Christian and the Muslim maintained the absolute transcendent reality of the one God who created heaven and earth and who made man in his own image and called him to share in his bliss but who could never be identified with him. Further, the Semitic religions maintained that man was separated from God not merely by an illusion of the mind, by 'ignorance', as in Hinduism, but by sin, by an aversion from the will of God, the absolute Good. Sin was not an illusion capable of being dispelled by knowledge, but a fault in human nature for which atonement had to be made. So it was that the Semitic religions offered a far better ground for realism. Nature and the world were real, and man and history had a meaning and a purpose in the mind of God. 'The divine action in the world was not merely an appearance of the one, eternal Being,' Father Bede would write, 'but an action of God in history which gives an ultimate meaning to human life. Time does not move in a cycle of rebirths as for the Hindu, but in a straight line towards a goal which is set before both the individual and the race.'

The doctrine of the one supreme personal God, who was infinitely holy and infinitely merciful; of a world which was created by God in total dependence on him and yet distinct from him, which was the sphere of good and evil forces; and the conception of history as having a purpose determined by God, according to which the entire creation was moving towards the time when it would be judged by God seemed to constitute a unique revelation, made originally to the Jews, on which both Christianity and Islam depended. This revelation gave a reality to nature and history and hence to science and to political life which was lacking in Hindu and Buddhist thought but which was better adapted to the contemporary world. Indeed, it was from this Semitic tradition that Father Bede saw the whole modern movement of science and humanism, of democracy and technology emerging and he could not envisage a way of going back on what had been gained in this way.

He was not unaware of the danger of a personal God being conceived in too human terms and becoming an image of a glorified man. Hence his reaction when Lewis many years earlier in his *Letters to Malcolm* had raised that crucial question, 'What soul ever perished for believing that God the Father really had a beard?' Against such an image the Hindu conception of the Brahman, the one, infinite, eternal Being, beyond speech and thought, of whom we can ultimately say no more than *neti, neti,* 'not this, not this', because the divine being transcends every image and conception of human thought, was of great and enduring value. If also when speaking of the person of God, the Christian meant a being of infinite wisdom and goodness whilst at the same time admitting that all these terms of person, being, wisdom and goodness could only be used by analogy because God transcends all human conception, then he was not far from the Hindu conception of *Saccidananda*, Being, Knowledge, Bliss which was yet beyond conception. The Christian had but to insist that in this Being of infinite mystery, the attributes of personal being really existed and were not mere appearances so that he could properly speak of personal relations, relations of knowledge and love within the absolute Being of the Godhead, according to the Christian doctrine of the Trinity, as well of personal relations between God and man.

Whereas Greek philosophy which had impressed itself so firmly upon Christianity started from the reality of this world and of man and led to the knowledge of God, Hindu philosophy started from the experience of the reality of God and sought to establish the reality of the world. The weakness in Hindu thought had been from the beginning, in Father Bede's view, that it had never been able to find a true relation between God, or the Absolute, and the relative world of time and space. Hindu doctrine could be divided into three schools: the Advaita school of the eighth century doctor Sankara and his way of knowledge or *jnana-marga*, which, in maintaining that the Absolute was one eternal, infinite, unchanging being, knowledge and bliss, was compelled to say that the world itself was *maya*. It had no reality in itself. Thus this world and the life of those who peopled it had no ultimate reality. The one ultimate was the Brahman, the infinite. By reaction, in the eleventh century Ramanuja with his 'way of devotion' known as *bhakti-marga* had tried to retain the reality of a personal God, of this world and of human souls and found himself compelled to regard the universe and souls as 'parts' or 'modes' of God and so fell into pantheism. A third school expounding the dualist or *Dvaita* philosophy, which might well have been influenced by Syrian Christianity since its leader Madhva came from Kerala, held that God, the world and souls were really distinct, but the world and souls were held to be eternal like God. Like all Indian systems it lacked the idea of creation and so could never resolve the problem of the relation of God to the world. It was Father Bede's conviction that by introducing the idea of creation and Christian incarnation, by showing Christ as true God and true man, uniting in his person 'without separation and without confusion' the two natures of God and man, Christian theology could bring the Vedanta to the goal which it had all along been seeking. This would not be to impose an alien theology on the Indian mind, but to show how Christ came to complete and perfect the age-long quest of the Indian mind for the knowledge of God.

  Hinduism was a religion of total interiority, interiority which consisted in a progressive detachment from everything both external and internal, leading to isolation of the soul in its pure interiority. It had no place for historical fact. It was also a religion which for all its depth of religious feeling and philosophical insight was inextricably bound up with mythology. The gods were symbols of the divine mystery, many of them profoundly significant, but they had no reality in themselves. Even Rama and Krishna, figures so central to Hindu devotion, were not truly historical figures. They were epic heroes who had been transformed into gods by the imagination of India. However beautiful and significant such figures might be, it was inevitable that as modern education spread, despite the existence of many who managed apparently without undue difficulty to combine much of western thought with Hindu worship, their reality would be called increasingly into question. Christ alone was capable of reconciling the ancient tradition of religion in India with the demands of the modern mind. Father Bede sought to convince Hinduism as once Tolkien and Dyson had convinced Lewis that in Christ myth and history had met. It was not enough that Christ should be looked upon as yet another symbolic figure like Rama or Krishna, as yet another *avatara* (divine incarnation). To Father Bede Christ was the fulfilment of all that the imagination of the Indian soul sought to find in its gods and heroes, in its sacrifices and its temples. Yet he was also a human being, who had entered into history, who had remained in his Church as a living power capable of transforming its economic and social and political life. It was when the Indian people recognized that Christ was in reality a historical figure, that he suffered, was crucified, died and was buried, that Christ was the point at which God entered history, not as a symbol but as a person, to change the course of history and transform it, that the decisive point in the history of India might also be reached.

What Father Bede envisaged was a meeting of religions 'in Christ'. Beginning from the fact that according to St Paul the whole creation took place 'in Christ', 'In him all things were created . . . all things were created through him and for him . . . and in him all things hold together' (Col. 1.16–17), the whole creation could be seen as a 'theophany', a manifestation of God; but this manifestation took place in Christ, and thus the whole creation became a manifestation of Christ. The Father manifested himself in his Son or Word, who by assuming human flesh assumed the whole creation to himself and filled it with his presence (Eph. 4.10). Thus nothing could properly be thought of apart from Christ; it was he who gave existence its meaning. At the same time Christ was the redeemer of the world. By taking human flesh he took the flesh of all mankind and redeemed human nature. There was therefore no one from the beginning to the end of the world who was not redeemed by him. It was in the light of this conception of Christ as the creator and redeemer and sanctifier of the world, who communicated his Spirit to man and enabled him to partake of the divine nature that Father Bede felt the whole problem of the religion (rather than the religions) of the world should be viewed.

The idea of a universal or 'cosmic' revelation which preceded all special forms of revelation, was basic to the biblical view of religion and was found in all Christian tradition. In the biblical view all men were originally included in God's plan of salvation. There was a solid tradition according to which Christianity, that is to say the mystery of Christ and the Church, could be said to have existed since the beginning of the world. It was present in creation, because the whole creation found its meaning and purpose in Christ who assumed the whole material universe into the life of God. It was present in all history because Christ came as the 'fulfilment' of history and revealed the nature of human destiny. Above all, it was found in the different religious traditions of the world because in them this 'mystery' was gradually unfolded. If Clement of Alexandria could find in Greek philosophy a 'preparation' for Christ like the Law for the Jews, how much more, argued Father Bede, was it possible to find such a 'preparation' in Hinduism, Buddhism, Taoism and Islam. In the Hindu concept of the Atman, the true Self of every man, who was one with the Brahman, the ultimate Reality; in the Buddhist concept of the Buddha – nature existing in all men; in the Taoist concept of the Tao as existing before all things and containing the meaning of all things; in the Muslim Sufi's concept of the Qutb, the 'pole' of the universe, who was also the Perfect Man; he discerned so many 'prophecies' of the mystery of Christ. From a Christian point of view there was no difficulty in perceiving Christ as the fulfilment of all religion. It was possible to say that the mystery of Christ was 'hidden' in all religion as it was hidden in Judaism, and that Christ himself came to reveal this hidden meaning, to make clear what was obscure, to make explicit what was implicit, to perfect what was imperfect.

In 1962, not insignificantly the year of the opening of the

Second Vatican Council which would bring support and confirmation to so much of what Father Bede had for some time been striving for, a meeting took place in Rajpur at the foot of the Himalayas at the invitation of the Swiss Ambassador to New Delhi, Dr Cuttat. The object of the meeting was to discuss the Christian approach to Hinduism; its conclusion was that the task was not so much to bring Christ to India, as to discover Christ already present and active in the Hindu soul. The question remained, however, as to whether a viewpoint that presented non-Christian religions as 'preparations' could ever be acceptable to people who were not Christians. Superficially such a prospect seemed unlikely. Yet Father Bede remained convinced that beneath the surface it was less so. All religion was after all in a state of continuous development and constant influence from outside. In each religion there was perhaps a vital principle, an inner law which enabled it to assimilate elements from outside while preserving its intrinsic character, but the evolution could not be questioned. Contemporary Hinduism with its temple worship and its various forms of devotion was very different from the early religion of the *Vedas*; Mahayana Buddhism with its conception of the Bodhisattva who refused to enter Nirvana until the whole world had been saved, was no less remote from the early Hinayana Buddhism; the mysticism of the great Sufis was an extraordinary development of the primitive faith of Islam. Similarly Christianity, whether of Catholicism or Orthodoxy, with its development of worship and theology and canon law, was a very different thing from the judaic Christianity of the early Church. In the light of the continuing evolution of all religions, by contact with the others an eventual 'meeting' was not impossible and in the process of growth Christianity, whilst not renouncing anything of the truth which it had received might well find the demands made upon it no less exacting than those made on other religions.

The fact that many people in the West were turning to Hinduism, Buddhism and Zen Buddhism, Father Bede saw as a consequence of the fact that they were seeking an experience which they were not finding in their own lives and very often did not find in Christianity, namely the experience of God in the depths of the soul. For the Hindu this experience was fundamental; to him it was the ultimate experience. The birth of Indian philosophy in the *Upanishads* came with the mystical experience by which the soul realized its identity with the Brahman *Tat twam asi* – Thou art That – in other words the soul in the ultimate ground of its being was one with the Brahman, the ultimate ground of all being. This was the experience which underlay all Hindu religion and philosophy and which Father Bede had found was sought no less earnestly in modern India than at any time in the past. The whole system of Yoga, with all its discipline of *asana* (posture), the *prauayama* (breathing), the control of the senses and the mind, was intended to bring the heart and the mind into a state in which it could, in the Hindu view at least, be absolutely one with God, with the 'ultimate reality'. In the West success in the material world, in building up a great civilization, had left people with a great sense of frustration, a feeling of emptiness within, a lack of reality, an inability to touch the inner centre of being where, as Father Bede would put it in an essay on the Church and Hinduism, 'we are at rest and where we can go to meet our fellow-men, go out to meet God, but to which we can always return'.

It was this centre which Father Bede felt that the West must find. The Hindu and the Buddhist had been seeking it all through the centuries in the East, and in a very real sense they had the secret of it. The Hindu experience of the inner centre where one was united with God, the ultimate reality, was, though it had various interpretations which might not be totally adequate, a very great thing. Jacques Maritain and other philosophers had explained it as ultimately an experience of the soul in its inmost depths; through which the individual got beyond the world of the senses, beyond his imagination, beyond all the world of thought, until he reached the inner centre where the soul was resting in itself. Maritain referred to it as an 'experience of the substantial being of the soul'. What Father Bede considered of additional importance was that the experience of the soul in its depths was not an experience of the soul alone. Indirectly at least God was encountered, the source of life, the source of being. Thus the Hindu experience (which the Buddhists also had, though in a somewhat different formulation) was really an experience of God in the sense of an experience of the absolute, the infinite, the eternal. Reading the ancient Hindu and Buddhist books Father Bede had a sense of genuine mystical experience. Passing beyond the barriers of the finite, the relative, and the temporal, the absolute was reached. What was lacking in Europe and America was precisely this inner dimension, an experience of the absolute which used to be fundamental.

The Hindu, the Buddhist, the oriental had this experience of an inner reality and it was very deeply related to the experience of God, though they might not call it that. While therefore Christianity could offer Hinduism a true relation between God, or the Absolute, and the relative world of time and space, Hinduism and Buddhism could help the West and the Christian Church which to some degree had followed the general trend of the West – not so much by techniques, although some might find these helpful, but by the whole orientation of their thought towards the centre of reality. If Christianity could point the way to fulfilment of the East, Christianity and the West could learn from the East the lesson of interiority. For centuries the western world had been making staggering progress in the exploration of the external world, but the time had come, in Father Bede's view, for the balance to be redressed. The West must learn again to explore the interior world. The Catholic Church had, of course, a long history in the exploration of that inner world and the experience of God. In the last centuries, however, it too had felt the pull of the times and its members had grown external in the practice of their religion. That was why already for many the discovery of the East, of Vedanta and Yoga and Zen had become the means of their awakening to the reality of the inner life. More widely still the Church as a whole was now engaged in a 'return to the sources'. Christians were seeking to recover the inner depth of their religion in the sources of Scripture, the liturgy and the Fathers.

Furthermore, if there was a genuine presence of the mystery of Christ in every religion then for non-Christian religions to find Christ did not mean their renunciation of their own truth, but on the contrary a discovery of it. For the non-Christian also it meant finding the hidden meaning of his own doctrine through all the stages of its evolution. It meant entering into the interior depth of the meaning of his scriptures to find their ultimate significance. So it was that Father Bede envisaged the ultimate nature of the 'meeting' of religions as a movement of 'return to the sources'. He saw it also as a meeting which must take place in the depths of the soul. To meet on the level of liturgy, of language, music and art was not unduly difficult. To meet on the level of philosophy and theology might be a more difficult and protracted task, although not one which he thought would be altogether impossible; but the real task of the Church, not only in India but in all the East where people still carried in their hearts the awareness of an inner reality, was to meet in the interior depths of the soul. It was said that in the experience of non-duality, *advaita* as the Hindus called it, a point was reached where differences disappeared. Surely it was in this inner centre that ultimately a true meeting could be achieved.

At Kurisumala Ashram Father Bede made a close study of Yoga as one of the six *darshanas* or systems of Hindu philosophy and what amounted to a scientific method of breaking through the world of the senses and separating the soul from its subjection to the body. Later, at Shantivanam he would eventually give up the practice of Yoga. Personally, he felt more interest in meditation and no longer experienced the same need for Yoga, but he would always remain grateful for the years he had spent doing regular *asanas*, acknowledging that perhaps if he had started earlier in life and therefore been more physically flexible, and perhaps if he had not begun to suffer from rheumatism he might have continued with it.

Now he meditates sitting in a chair, stressing that he is always interested in not being too oriental in relating to the West and that he would not like to give the impression that it is only possible to meditate seated on the ground. He has retained a great interest in Kundalini Yoga which meets the needs both of his sense of belonging in a realm 'beyond' and of the transformation of energy, for it is a form of meditation which is not of the head but of the heart and not only of the heart but of the whole body and the breath. Through Kundalini Yoga he would learn how the energies could be channelled from the base of the spine, from the physical being through the sex energy, through the emotions, how they could be raised up and could eventually go beyond. Kundalini, the 'Serpent Power', the divine Power or *Shakti* conceived as lying coiled at the base of the spine, could be drawn up through the various *chakras* or centres of psychic energy until the *Shakti* (the feminine power) united with Shiva (the masculine power of consciousness) in the top of the head and the whole being was integrated with the divine. At Kurisumala Father Francis Mahieu was very committed to Yoga and a Yogi came regularly to the ashram to give the community instruction.

The ashram was flourishing. The monks found themselves able to extend their land and at their initiative a number of cooperative dairy farms had been started nearby. The community grew in time to incorporate twenty young monks and Father Bede found himself giving a complete course in theology to six of them. Study and instruction absorbed him for ten years and for ten years he and Father Francis agreed perfectly. Yet there was a slight divergence of viewpoints. Father Francis was very much absorbed in a Syrian thesis and would eventually embark upon an enormously comprehensive translation of the Syrian liturgy in five volumes, in Father Bede's view a wonderful work but one which, including as it did only a little material from the *Upanishads*, represented something of a diversion from their original objective. They had come to India to experience the Indian culture. The Syrian interest, though beautiful and impressive, was not the primary end. Father Francis was in Father Bede's eyes a very good, capable and deep man, one whom for ten years he accepted very readily as his superior. Yet he was also a very dominating character who was reluctant to devolve authority. In the end it was a mutual friend, a Belgian visitor to the ashram, who expressed the view that Father Francis should perhaps share his authority more. Father Bede very innocently passed the suggestion on only to find that it upset his superior greatly. Father Francis, apparently believing that Father Bede was trying to undermine his authority, took a year's sabbatical to think about it, but at the end of the year the wound had still not healed and Father Bede, unforgiven, had almost reached a point where he felt that he could no longer remain at Kurisumala. Providentially it was 1968, the year in which Henri Le Saux had finally decided that he could not continue to return at intervals to Shantivanam from his hermitage in the north of India. Le Saux felt more at home in the north, he found the travelling between the two places increasingly tiring and the upkeep of the ashram in his absence was expensive. He and Father Francis had been close for many years and so when Abhishiktananda left Shanti-vanam it was only natural that he should entrust it to Father Francis Mahieu. For a while the question was weighed as to which of the two founders of Kurisumala Ashram should go to Shantivanam and eventually Father Francis chose to remain in Kerala. The move to Saccidananda Ashram was something which in his very old age Father Bede would not regret.

Saccidananda Ashram

Father Bede's first days at Saccidananda Ashram were by no means easy. He arrived to bring new life to the cluster of huts, the small oratory and the guest house beside the Cauvery river initially together with two other brothers from Kurisumala, but neither of his two companions stayed. One returned to Kurisumala after a relatively short time; the other went to a seminary to study theology but when he had nearly completed the course decided to marry. He was, in Father Bede's view 'an intelligent chap', the marriage was a happy one and he appeared to have found the right way, but his leaving left Father Bede very much on his own. Father Francis sent one more brother from Kurisumala but he too returned after about six months and the superior at Kurisumala became ever more doubtful of the possibility of building up a community at Shantivanam and ever more reluctant to send support. There was a time when Father Bede found himself totally alone on the ashram but for a manager who himself would prove the cause of many difficulties. Now Father Bede makes light of the periods when he felt the ashram and the community he envisaged must come to an end. During those periods he undoubtedly knew what it was to be disappointed and discouraged but they would also teach him the importance of surrendering his hopes and aspirations to a higher authority: 'More than once I have surrendered the whole thing. That's the secret. If you really renounce somehow it comes itself.' Somehow he managed to preserve the conviction that there was something at work in Saccidananda Ashram, a conviction reinforced in the course of time by the fact that many people seemed to be drawn there as if by inspiration. The first of these were two more Indian brothers from Kurisumala Ashram, Amaldas and Cristudas whom he had known before he left for Shantivanam.

Seated cross-legged on the veranda outside his hut in an area of cultivated garden which is reserved for the brothers and into which guests may enter only by invitation, Amaldas would recall his first arrival at Kurisumala Ashram. Amaldas had been attracted from a very early age to the *sannyasi* life, inspired mainly by films he had seen of the life of John the Baptist, of the Desert Fathers and of Yogis living in the forest. Despite such fleeting insights, however, he had arrived at the ashram on the Kerala hillside with little idea of what life there would really entail. Confronted by the imposing figures of Father Francis and Father Bede at work but unspeaking in their carefully preserved Cistercian silence he had felt himself to be in the presence of saints, and he had remained. He had shown a particular interest in meditation and yoga exercises. Father Bede had taught him some *asanas*, then another brother had given him further instruction. When visitors from Yoga schools elsewhere came to the ashram he had been particularly eager to learn. Yet at Kurisumala the day's schedule had barely allowed for the practice of private prayer and meditation. The brothers had risen at 3.45 a.m., from 4 − 5 a.m. there had been community prayer, from 5 − 6 Bible reading and reflection, from 6 − 7 further community worship, breakfast then work and study. Amaldas had found the hour between 5 and 6 a.m. insufficient for both Bible reading and meditation. He developed the habit of rising even earlier to do his exercises. The brothers slept in dormitories but Amaldas was assistant guestmaster. He would find himself a vacant guest room or go and sit on a rock outside.

On one occasion, meditating on top of a rock, he had lost all sense of time, and the entire community had turned out to search for him. On another, in 1970, after his *Brahmachariya diksha* – his first profession, he had gone to Sabarimala forest in Kerala to spend forty days in prayer and fasting with only one meal a day. In the very early hours of the morning a wild elephant had thrust its trunk through the window of the *sataram* or inn where he was sleeping. Afraid because the huge animal could so easily break through the fragile walls of the room, he had nevertheless begun to sing 'OM *Nama Christaya*' (adoration to Christ). At a loss for any other assistance he had placed his complete trust in Christ: 'Suddenly an inner voice told me, if Jesus Christ is so close to me, closer than myself, if my body is Jesus Christ's body and my blood is Jesus Christ's blood, then why to fear? He is more powerful than the elephant.' The elephant had remained at the window for a while listening to the singing then left without harming the singer. Throughout that night Amaldas remained awake singing the name of Jesus. To him it seemed as if he had been granted a direct experience of the fact that the name of Jesus was more powerful than the elephant.

Amaldas' conviction that he was called to give more time to meditation had grown ever stronger. He had put to Father Francis his vision of a monastic life in which the daytime could be devoted to community prayer and activity but the night to individual contemplative life. He had suggested that he should attend morning prayer and the Mass and work in the ashram until noon but that he should then be free to pass the afternoon and night in private meditation in a hut set apart from the community. Despite the fact that he was reluctant to lose one of the more senior and committed members of the ashram and despite the fact that he had been prepared to grant Amaldas a certain amount of lee-way, Father Francis' reaction to the proposition was one of indignation. If Amaldas was not prepared to abide by the rules of the ashram, he must start his own. Amaldas had stayed on at Kurisumala for a while but his problem arose again and again. Since Father Francis was his superior he had not been particularly close to Father Bede at Kurisumala but he had always felt a special affection for him. When Father Bede left for Saccidananda Ashram Amaldas had deliberated for some time with regard to what he should give the older man as a memento of his affection. Finally he settled upon a triangle of white paper in the centre of which Father Bede, when he received it, wrote the single word 'OM'. Amaldas had asked

Father Bede if he might accompany him then, but the response had been that for the moment he must remain where he was. Later perhaps he could come. It was some time later at a juncture when Father Bede must have felt himself deserted that he received a letter from Amaldas and Cristudas asking to join him at Saccidananda Ashram.

Cristudas, too, had felt himself ill-suited to the daily routine at Kurisumala which left many of the brothers exhausted and which had induced even Father Bede to fall asleep on occasions during the Mass. He too felt a special attachment to Father Bede. At the age of twelve he had had what he would later regard as a 'direct revelation of an all-embracing love', a dream in which he had fallen into a deep well. None of his family or friends were able to rescue him from his agony but then there appeared the figure of a man with very long arms who reached down into the well and with the words, 'Come my son,' lifted him out of the depths. Some years later Cristudas had written to Father Francis asking to spend a week's retreat at Kurisumala Ashram. He had arrived in what had seemed to him to be an extraordinarily beautiful setting at a time when the brothers were at prayer. In the tall but stooping figure of Father Bede with his very long arms and one foot slightly twisted from the ill-fitting shoes he had worn in his youth, Cristudas identified the rescuer of his dream. His adolescent vision had prefigured Father Bede in every detail and from the moment when he first fell at the stranger's feet to receive his blessing he had felt that he belonged at his side. He was and would remain 'mad after Father Bede, his holiness and compassion'. When, in response to the Indian brothers' letter, Father Bede wrote back from Saccidananda Ashram that they would be welcome and that he would take care of them as if they were his sons, Cristudas perceived in the reply an echo and the fulfilment of his dream.

When Amaldas finally left Kurisumala for Saccidananda Ashram it was really an act of disobedience. He had informed Father Francis and the community that he would return after a short period but he never actually did so. Father Bede had given his assurance that at Saccidananda Ashram the main community prayer was only held three times a day. Amaldas could have a hut to himself and the entire night would be his for private meditation. There would be difficulties and problems in the years that followed. At one time Amaldas left Shantivanam to spend three months in the north considering the idea of starting his own ashram but his conscience and sense of responsibility prevailed: 'Because I don't want to face the situation I am going to start another ashram. It is my responsibility to build the existing ashram up.' In any case, no sooner had he set foot outside Saccidananda Ashram than he experienced a 'strong current of vibrations' from Father Bede. Six months after Amaldas' first appearance at Shantivanam, Cristudas followed him. Father Francis, still reluctant to lose promising members of his community to Saccidananda Ashram, had succeeded in dissuading him for a while, but in the end the bond with Father Bede proved to be too strong.

It was a bond that would be further strengthened by time and one which Father Bede himself would look upon as extraordinary. Yet the dream experience was one which he recognized as not uncommon, particularly amongst Hindus. A Brazilian lady had once told him of how someone had appeared to her in a dream asking her to translate his work into Portuguese. It had taken her some time to discover that the dream figure was Ramana Maharshi. The whole of the psychic world Father Bede has found to be much more present in India. It is a world which fascinates him in a way, but he himself purports not to have psychic experiences despite the Welsh blood on his father's side, a fact for which he is thankful because to be psychic is a dubious gift and one so easily confused with the spiritual. Yet the existence of the great psychic world and the experiences connected with it are things which he finds no difficulty in accepting: the materializations effected by Sai Baba, for example, or the process by which the Shiva lingam grows within the body of Swami Premananda and eventually issues from his mouth as a beautiful little statue.

Father Bede has no doubt that there is subtle matter which can be formed in this way and that some people are very sensitive to this subtle element. Between the physical world and the spiritual world, the world of divine reality, there is the psychic or astral world. Hindu tradition distinguishes between gross senses and subtle senses and gross matter and subtle matter. These subtle senses are present in all men but in most people today they are not developed. The modern scientific habit of mind has led to a concentration on gross matter and its rational analysis. Yet the evidence of the existence of this 'psychic world' accumulates continually. When Christ performed his miracles he was, in Father Bede's view, demonstrating not only the power of God but the powers latent in human nature. These powers, or *siddhis* have a long history in India and are the recognized result of the advanced practice of Yoga. Father Bede sees these powers as in themselves good for they are created by God, manifestations of the divine *Shakti*. To him there are angels present everywhere and when the angel is subject to the law of God it becomes an instrument of God in the universe. When, however, it centres on itself, making itself its own law, it becomes a power of conflict and disorder, a demonic power. What Father Bede is further at pains to stress is that it is important to distinguish between the physical, the psychic and the spiritual. In India when people visit a holy man they do so in order to receive a *darshan*. It is a source of embarrassment to Father Bede when they prostrate themselves at his feet and call him God: 'What they really mean is "God is in you".'

By the time Father Bede moved to Saccidananda Ashram he had been wearing *kavi*, the colour of *sannyasi* dedication, for some ten years and he had found himself accepted as a *sannyasi*. Very early on in his Indian life he remembers attending a meeting between Christians and Hindus and entering a room to be warmly welcomed by about a dozen *sannyasis*. In renouncing the world a *sannyasi* ceases to belong to any social state. In principle *sannyasa* is beyond all religious divisions. That in practice he should have found himself so readily respected and accepted remains grounds for his own high regard for Indian *sannyasis*. Despite such ready acceptance, however, it took time for his understanding of India and the Indian psychology to mature. Amaldas and Cristudas would look back on the Father Bede they had known at Kurisumala as one who for all his compassion was, in their view, very strict and one who aligned himself with the idea that 'provided you attended the community prayers, did your manual work conscientiously and kept silence you were a good monk'.

The Father Bede they had known then would not allow them to spend their rest period in the garden but insisted that they rested in the dormitory in case, if allowed to remain outside, they talked. Nor would he allow them to lie on their beds to rest wearing only their *dhotis*. They must cover themselves with a *kurta* or shirt. Now Father Bede himself often leaves his chest uncovered. He attributes the Indian brothers' early impression of him as strict partly to the fact that he had been trained in the Benedictine tradition of obedience and partly to the simple fact of his being English, which meant that he lived more by his reason than the average Indian. It was part of his cultural inheritance to control his feelings; no such inhibitions prevailed amongst his Indian brothers. Community meetings at Kurisumala were chaotic, heated and even violent affairs compared with the quiet order of Benedictine Chapter meetings. In the villages tremendous quarrels could erupt quite suddenly and just as suddenly subside. There was no escaping the realization that if on the whole the way in which the people of India lived from the emotions meant that they were affectionate and loving and beautiful, it also meant that they were at times angry and resentful and desperate for revenge. The same people who created the most warm and attractive family life could also be readily roused to bloodshed. There was a dark side to charm which took the form of manipulation – and there was, as I had witnessed in the place of sacrifice in the Kalighat, a dark side to Hinduism. In Bangalore a fit young man had been compelled to take refuge in a tree to escape being offered as a human sacrifice. The mothers of Shantivanam went through a period of frantic concern for the safety of their children when a local bridge was under construction. In order to make the bridge safe it was believed necessary to bury a live baby in it. The sense of the sacred itself was ambivalent. Father Bede saw it as something operating at a rather deep level in the Indian people. Right from infancy they became accustomed to rituals and ceremonies which could become somewhat superficial as they grew older yet he felt that a genuine sense of the sacred prevailed on many levels. What he did concede was that this same sense of the sacred was compatible with extreme immorality, violence and many other 'vices'. It was not to be automatically equated with the holy but belonged rather to the psychic world which must ideally be assumed into the spiritual. Thus the task of Christianity might be seen as one of purifying the sacred.

With the passage of the years his understanding of the Indian psychology would penetrate deeper and deeper until Father Bede felt it was an inalienable part of him, and doubtless the need to integrate into his vision the negative aspects of the land and the people with whom he felt so at one contributed to his growth. By the time he took over Saccidananda Ashram he had been in India for over thirteen years, years which had in some way opened and broadened him. During the ensuing years he would continue to change and with him the ashram would change also. Father Bede had been and undoubtedly would remain deeply influenced by the two founders of the ashram and their book *An Indian Benedictine Ashram*, and he would always retain a sense of continuing their work, but in the years following the Second Vatican Council the Church and society changed so rapidly and so substantially that it would have been inappropriate to follow exactly what they had envisaged. Father Monchanin had belonged very much to the ascetic tradition of a life of austerity in renunciation of the world, so much so that he had virtually killed himself by excessive fasting and hardship. On the strength of his own personal experience perhaps, this was not a lifestyle that Father Bede on the whole encouraged. His

own youth had taught him the dangers of obsessive fasting
and too much silence. Jules Monchanin and Henri Le Saux
had themselves differed in the degree to which they had been
open to the oriental tradition. Father Monchanin had worked
out what Father Bede would consider a very beautiful
theology and one which would still be highly respected in
Europe but which was not perhaps sufficiently open to the
movement of change as it developed after his death. Father Le
Saux had gone more deeply into the Hindu experience to the
point of quarrelling with his companion and accusing him of
being a Greek with a dialectical mind. Again, Father Bede
differed from Le Saux in that the latter went deep into the
Hindu experience of *Advaita* and beyond it to what he called
the 'acosmic state'. The objective, as Le Saux saw it, was for
the individual gradually to free himself from all bonds until he
reached pure *Advaita*, non-duality beyond; Father Bede's
idea was for the individual to endeavour to detach himself
from the outer world and from the self but in his view when
this point of the spirit was reached the dynamism of love
could be encountered. Thus it was not just a question of
'going beyond' but of attaining that point at which the
individual was totally open to the Spirit. The Spirit might
then call him not necessarily to total withdrawal from the
world but to the life of a Mother Teresa amongst the very
poorest of the poor.

Father Bede's conception of a *sannyasi* was along similar
lines: a *sannyasi* went beyond all social states, beyond all
religion, but having done so he could of his own freedom
under the guidance of the Spirit unite himself with a particular
community or congregation. Both Le Saux and Monchanin
had seen the ashram very much as a place of contemplation
separated from the world, placing a very strong emphasis on
silence, and there had been a time when Father Bede would
have shared that view. At Prinknash the life of prayer led
within the confines of a monastery from which he had hardly
emerged for fifteen years had seemed to him the ideal,
although even then there had been moments when he had felt
that he was not sharing enough. Still when he first came to
India his aim had been to create a contemplative monastery in

which to live. At Shantivanam which was much more of an Indian ashram the life had naturally become less Cistercian and more Benedictine. Later he would feel rather strongly that each person should have the space in which to develop himself within the context of the community life. What would become a strong conviction was already latent when first he had made Amaldas welcome at the ashram. He was being led outwards from his original view and the message of Indian interiority in the fullest sense would not elude him. Silence was something to be created within, and not necessarily imposed from without, something which could be maintained without physical separation from the turmoil of the world. The deep inner silence of the ashram was something which the world could be invited to share and which the brothers could carry out to the world.

Fathers Monchanin and Le Saux had not made any attempt at the cultivation of land but when Amaldas and Cristudas arrived, on the strength of their experience of farming the ostensibly infertile hillsides of Kurisumala, they began to manure the ground thoroughly and planted tomatoes and beans. With a plentiful supply of cow dung the crops flourished. In time they would acquire a number of cows and find themselves in a position to devote two or three acres to paddy which was sufficient to provide them with three crops a year for the needs of the ashram and grow a variety of fruit and vegetables. Part of some land given to them by the government the community cultivated in association with a neighbouring *Harijan* village and the villagers shared in the produce. The ashram would also establish close contact with the villagers through a dispensary and two nursery schools which they helped to establish in neighbouring villages and which provided the children with a midday meal. A small but steady flow of visitors to the ashram must be provided with hospitality. With the help of local labourers and craftsmen a wing was added to the three-roomed guesthouse. Father Bede himself designed a new octagonal shaped library constructed with a veranda in attractive local tiles to replace the small room which his predecessors had used to harbour

their predominantly French literature behind the wire mesh-
ing necessary to keep the wildlife at bay, and local carpenters
worked through the night to complete the roof.

Such expansion was undertaken with the idea of preserving
the original pattern of the cluster of huts among the palmyra
palms. It was also undertaken in the face of many difficulties.
Some of these appear to have been the direct consequence of
the very same qualities which attracted people to the ashram:
Father Bede's capacity not to stand in judgement and to see
only the good. In the eyes of his two companions, Amaldas
and Cristudas, such qualities, though Christlike, could also
be infuriatingly impractical. Father Bede's readiness to allow
people the freedom and the space in which to recognize for
themselves the error of their ways was undoubtedly the
product of his gentleness and compassion. It also verged
dangerously upon the openness to exploitation to which so
many of his fellow countrymen were prone: 'The English in
general have that believing kind of attitude. Indians have very
crooked minds but you don't see that. We use your simplicity
and sincerity.' It is not a subject which Father Bede would
wish to pursue but on numerous occasions his trust was
abused: a weaver who had been provided with a loom to work
on the ashram went off with all the money he could steal, one
manager at Saccidananda Ashram subjected him to all kinds
of deceit, another whom Father Bede left in charge of the cooperative dairy farms at Kurisumala during Father Francis'
absence had cheated him out of substantial sums. In the more
pragmatic view of Cristudas whose task it was to balance the
books at Shantivanam, administration was not Father Bede's
strong point. In fact, he was not very practical in general. In
Gospel terms he was very decidedly not Martha but Mary.
With the passage of the years Cristudas would come more to
share Father Bede's attitude with regard to not worrying
unduly about the morrow – countless examples of 'the Lord
providing' would lend it powerful credence – and he would
recognize in Father Bede's evident lack of concern about
material things a mark of holiness, the putting into practice of
the detachment he preached. In the early stages of building up

Saccidananda Ashram, however, that lack of practicality and his reluctance to say no to anyone was the cause of certain tensions. But then tensions, according to Father Bede, provide the stimulus for growth.

There were other problems. Rumours ran rife in the locality as to what went on in the ashram. There were suggestions of immorality amongst a good deal of other speculation. Furthermore, the successor to Bishop Mendonca, the bishop who had stood so unequivocally behind Jules Monchanin's and Henri Le Saux's endeavours, was not so sympathetic to the ashram's cause. Monchanin and Le Saux had not had any formal monastic status. They had simply formed a community under the local bishop. Father Bede and his companions on the other hand had retained their monastic status under Kurisumala and were thus only answerable to the local bishop with regard to the liturgy used. Strictly speaking they were still Syrian monks and yet they were in a Latin diocese. The first brothers were Malayalis towards whom Tamils feel a long-standing hostility, and their Superior was a foreigner. The bishop was very keen that Tamil should be incorporated into the Indian liturgy and resented the intrusion from Kerala. A potentially inflammatory situation was further fuelled by what the bishop considered to be experimentation at the personal whim of the English *sannyasi*. When Father Bede first moved to Saccidananda Ashram he celebrated the Mass of the Syrian rite translated into English but Sanskrit was used increasingly. The community evolved a form of worship which included readings from the *Vedas*, the *Upanishads* and the *Bhagavad Gita* as well as from the Tamil classics and other scriptures together with psalms and readings from the Bible. Sanskrit as well as Tamil *bhajans* were sung accompanied by drums and cymbals. The practice of *arati*, the waving of lights before the blessed Sacrament, was carried out together with other Indian customs which would become generally accepted in the Church in India. On more than one occasion the bishop tried to put a stop to the rite used in the ashram but Father Bede appealed to the liturgical commission in India which gave him its support.

In fairness to the bishop Father Bede would be quick to

point out that he and others in the diocese who reacted unfavourably and at times even cruelly against members of the ashram were frequently on the receiving end of wild stories about what it stood for. The impression amongst more conservative Christians who failed to look beyond the architecture and practices more readily associated with Hindu tradition to their significance within the Christian tradition was that the community was following Hinduism not Christianity. They looked at the *gopuram* or gateway to the temple and saw the three-headed figure which according to Hindu tradition represented the three aspects of the Godhead as Creator, Preserver and Destroyer of the universe but failed to recognize in that same figure the image of the Holy Trinity shown emerging from the cross as an indication that the mystery of the Trinity was revealed through the cross of Christ. Attacks written by traditionalist Catholics appeared in the press. One organization in particular which stood for Catholicism in its pre-Second Vatican Council form and was financed from the United States wrote articles in its publications denouncing the ashram as heretical and urging the bishop to close it down. A journalist accompanying a Jesuit priest who visited the ashram, to whom Father Bede with characteristic trust spoke very freely, compiled an article making a mockery of everything that Saccidananda Ashram stood for. People who actually joined the ashram proved to be insincere and dishonest in their motives. An Indian priest with a degree from England who was teaching in an Indian university department devoted to the study of Christianity, Sikhism, Hinduism and Buddhism seemed to Father Bede to be ideally suited to membership of the ashram until he began making moves to persuade Amaldas and Cristudas that as Malayalis they were not welcome there. It later transpired that under the guise of friendship he was attempting to take over the ashram and almost certainly acting on the directions of the bishop. Experiences of this kind about which Father Bede would be reluctant to speak must have wounded him deeply and did bring him to acknowledge that the Indian people, for all their great 'sympathy' could be exasperating.

On more than one occasion he considered leaving. In so many ways the work was very precarious, but the periods of desolation were periods which, in retrospect at least, he would regard as necessary for growth. They would teach him to live on the basis of faith that 'something was coming through' and not to become too disturbed by opposition and apparent failure.

Fortunately, despite the criticism that at times found its way as far afield as Rome, there was also support. The local villagers, for all their inbuilt rejection of Malayalis, were brought into contact with the ashram through the work it provided and generally reacted favourably towards its Indian character. In 1975 the community would replace the flat roof of the temple with a *vimana*, a dome in the style of local Hindu temples. Together with Jyoti Sahi, a Catholic artist from Bangalore, Father Bede toured a number of villages to gather ideas and, with the help of Hindu craftsmen, over the inner sanctuary of the temple at Saccidananda Ashram a *vimana* was erected. On the simple stone altar in the *garbha griha* the blessed sacrament was reserved. The sacrament signified the mystery of the death and resurrection of Christ through which the worshipper was able to pass through death to resurrection and eternal life. The *vimana* above the sanctuary was to represent the ascent to the 'new creation' through the resurrection. Thus at its base were depicted the four beasts of the Apocalypse (Rev. 4.7), the lion, the ox, the man and the eagle, representing the whole creation redeemed by Christ. Above them were four saints, representing redeemed humanity, and above them four figures of Christ in different postures seated on a royal throne and surrounded by angels. To the east was the figure of Christ as king and beneath him the figure of the Virgin Mary as Queen of heaven clothed with the sun, and with the moon and the stars at her feet (Rev. 12.1), treading on the serpent. To the north was Christ as priest in the *abhaya mudra* taking away fear and conferring grace and beneath him St Peter with the keys to the kingdom of heaven. To the south was Christ as prophet or teacher in the attitude of a teacher or guru and beneath him St Paul as teacher of the nations. Finally, to the west was Christ as contemplative in the *dhyana* or meditation position and beneath him St Benedict, the founder of contemplative life in the West. Above these figures of Christ and the saints was the throne of God represented by a dome covered with peacock feathers and above this again was the lotus, symbol of purity supporting the *kalasam* an ancient symbol of the four elements pointing upwards to the *akasa*, the infinite space where God dwells in 'inaccessible light'. Just as at the entrance to the temple the *gopuram* was designed to direct the mind to the mystery of the Godhead as three persons adored by angels, so as the worshipper drew nearer through the mystery of the Cross and the Resurrection he was invited to contemplate the 'new heaven and the new earth' which was the destiny of man and beyond this the ineffable mystery of the Godhead beyond name and form to which all earthly images are intended to lead.

Considerable thought and attention to detail went into the design and construction of the *vimana* to the extent that when it was discovered, after the initial plans had been made, that in a Hindu temple the figure of Shiva as guru always faces south, the original position of Christ the prophet and of St Paul was changed so that they too could face south. When the time came for the *vimana* to be consecrated the bishop was initially reluctant to grant his permission for a ceremony which would be very much along Hindu lines. Eventually he agreed to be present but on the very day on which the consecration was to take place, when the welcoming banners were already in position, he sent word that he would be unable to attend. In the end he did send a representative and about 5,000 people from all the local villages took part in a ceremony of consecration in which Father Bede and Amaldas climbed a specially constructed ramp to pour water over the top of the *vimana*. Once anointed in this way it would acquire for the local people a very sacred character and almost invariably when they passed they would thereafter pay reverence to it. Inevitably the *vimana* provoked criticism among those who saw it as being more Hindu than Christian but the growth of the ashram became more evident. The temple roof would be further extended, a new and larger refectory would be built, the number of guest rooms would be increased with individual huts for those seeking more solitude, and in time Amaldas would design a circular meditation hall used for Yoga classes and silent meditation. About a year after the consecration of the *vimana* the opportunity to have a woman join the community arose. Ten years later Father Bede would suggest that the ashram would be more open to the idea of women as permanent members but at the time it did not seem appropriate. Marie Louise decided nonetheless to purchase some land a little further along the bank of the Cauvery and an ashram would grow up spontaneously around her where guests staying for longer periods or wanting greater seclusion could find accommodation, and where she would prepare Indian girls either for marriage or for the religious life.

A number of people came to join the small community at Shantivanam. 'All of them', to use Father Bede's words, 'good in different ways', but for a variety of reasons, 'not entirely satisfactory'. For many Indians it was not easy to live with the flow of western visitors who passed through with their western ways and their apparent relative wealth which did not fail to fascinate. Potential permanent members of the ashram came, experimented and left in a manner which Father Bede found not exactly disturbing but not at all encouraging. There were periods of darkness, but then it was in darkness that God was to be found. Dionysius had spoken of the divine darkness. St Gregory of Nyssa had presented the journey of Israel through the desert as culminating in Moses going up to meet God in the darkness, in the cloud of Mount Sinai. When a worshipper came to the inner sanctuary of a Hindu temple, he came to his own heart, to the inner centre of his own being, where he encountered God without form in darkness. Really, the journey towards God was a journey into the unconscious, for it was deep in the unconscious, beyond all imagery or thought, that God was hidden.

12

Beyond all Concepts of the Rational Mind

Despite the increasing evidence that 'something was coming through', there were occasions when even Father Bede would admit the stress was very great. The stomach pains from which he had suffered at Kurisumala had eventually been diagnosed as tubercular enteritis and for some time he received treatment for that. Later an irregular heartbeat meant a period in the German-run St Thomas' hospital and further treatment. If those close to Father Bede are able to find any fault with him it is associated not only with his readiness to trust but with a tendency to be irritated, largely, it should be said, by those who speak ill of others, an excessive readiness to make himself available to anyone who wishes to see him, and a propensity to overwork. Amidst all the daily preoccupations of the ashram Father Bede found time to study, to give lectures and to write. His writing bore witness possibly to a desire to clarify the position of Saccidananda Ashram to the increasing number of people who showed an interest in it and in him, and certainly to his continuing consideration of Hindu and Christian philosophy in the light of the challenge presented to them both by modern science and secularism. Could it not be that this very challenge could enable both religions to come to a deeper understanding of the implications of their faith and in doing so to meet and enrich one another? 'Can the Vedanta learn from Christian faith, as it has learned from the different currents of Saivite and Vaishnavite faith, which it has encountered in the course of its history, and so develop along new lines?' asked Father Bede in a series of lectures in 1973 that would subsequently be made into a book entitled

Vedanta and Christian Faith. 'And can the Christian faith, which first elaborated its philosophy through contact with Greek thought, be brought now into vital contact with the Vedanta, and so develop a new system of philosophy and discover new implications of doctrine?'

He had identified a crisis in the West relating to the problem of the existence of God, which he saw as arising very largely from the fact that the original Hebrew revelation of God, whilst conceiving of him as a 'hidden God' dwelling in cloud and darkness, had been given very largely in anthropomorphic terms. The Hebrew conceived of God as above all a Person, a moral Being, who was known by his action in history and his providence over the life both of nations and individuals. The Hebrew also thought in images not in concepts and his representation of God, which Father Bede recognized as legitimate if properly understood, was never analysed philosophically. The Greek Fathers of the Church, who had inherited the metaphysical mind of the Greeks, had been able to correct this tendency until eventually St Thomas Aquinas had formulated what, in Father Bede's view, represented the most adequate conception of God which the human mind had ever achieved. Yet even this conception had now come under attack, partly because of the prejudice against metaphysical thought which the scientific mind tended to produce, partly because the metaphysical conception of God tended to be mistaken for the reality and so the concept of God became an 'idol' no less than the image, whereas in fact, as Aquinas had well understood all language about God was necessarily analogical. Even to say that God existed was to speak in terms of analogy since God's mode of existence was quite different from that of any other being. Of God it was only possible to say what he was not; what he was could never properly be expressed.

For modern man both the image and the metaphysical concept had broken down. He was now faced with the ultimate mystery of God before which speech and thought were silent and it was here that Father Bede felt that India had a message for the contemporary world. India had never been so preoccupied with images and concepts of God as had western man. In India it had been understood from the very beginning that God could not properly be imagined or conceived. The *Upanishads* were not philosophical treatises or speculations about the nature of God or the universe like the writings of the contemporary Greek philosophers. They were the record of an experience intended to lead others to the same experience. The Indian mind had never been content to know 'about' God, it had always sought to know God, to 'realize' him, to experience his presence not in the imagination or in the intellect but in the 'ground' or substance of the soul, from which all the faculties sprang. The seers of the *Upanishads* had sought to penetrate beyond the senses and beyond rational thought to the hidden mystery which lay 'behind' and 'within' everything. Behind all the appearances of the visible world was the one reality of the Brahman, and behind all the appearances of the body with its imagination and its thought was the reality of the Atman, the Self, and this underlying reality was known not by reasoning but by direct experience. The Self was experienced in its own 'ground', in the substance of its being, and knew itself in its identity with the 'ground' or substance of the universe. The *Upanishads* approached the divine mystery by way of affirmation using images and symbols to represent it; then by negation because ultimately it was only possible to say of the divine mystery *neti, neti* (Br.Up.2.3.6) 'not this, not this'.

Yet if negation was the primary way of expressing the mystery there was nonetheless one affirmation, which though inevitably inadequate, pointed to it more clearly than any other: the term *saccidananda*. The ultimate reality, the ultimate truth was *sat* – being, *cit* – knowledge, or consciousness, as Father Bede by this time preferred to call it, and *ananda* - bliss. The *Katha Upanishad* clearly affirmed that the divine mystery was Being but the 'being' that was affirmed of the Godhead was not being in the ordinary sense, it was not the being of the logician or the philosopher. It was the transcendent mystery of being, beyond speech or thought, an idea which Father Bede had derived many years earlier from a passage by Coleridge:

Hast thou ever raised thy mind to the consideration of existence in and by itself, as the mere act of existing? Hast thou ever said to thyself thoughtfully, It is! heedless at that moment whether it were a man before you or a flower or a grain of sand, without reference in short to this or that particular mode or form of existence? If thou hast indeed attained to this, then thou wilt have felt the presence of a mystery which must have fixed thy spirit in awe and wonder . . . If thou hast mastered this intuition of absolute existence, then thou wilt have learned likewise that it was this and no other which in early ages seized the nobler minds, the elect among men with a sacred horror. This it was which first caused them to feel in themselves something infinitely greater than our individual nature.

It was this same intuition of being, of the mystery of existence, which underlay Hindu thought, but this very mystery was apprehended not as a concept as in Greek thought but as an experience. Being was experienced in consciousness of Being, not as the object but as the subject of thought, the ground alike of being and of thought. The mind transcended all images and concepts and knew itself in the very ground of its being and in doing so discovered the infinity of Being in which it was grounded. It knew itself in the source of its being and of all being, in the source of all matter and life and consciousness. It discovered the identity of the Brahman and the Atman, the source of being both of the universe and of the self, the ultimate truth, the ultimate reality; and the consciousness of being in non-duality was the source of endless bliss in which all desires were satisfied.

The mystical experience revealed in the *Upanishads* was not without very evident relation to the religious and philosophical experience of the West for though the Hebrew had habitually conceived God as a Person and had not hesitated to use anthropomorphic language about him, he had, argued Father Bede, always retained the sense of the divine being as a mystery. Similarly in the New Testament, though God was referred to as a Father in the closest intimacy with man, the sense of mystery was always present. 'No man has ever seen God' said St John. Nevertheless in the New Testament as in the Old, God was conceived in relation to man. It was left to the Greek Fathers to speculate about the divine nature itself. For them it was an axiom that God was beyond all description and could not be properly named, and it was only in the sixth century that the Syrian monk who wrote under the name of Dionysius the Areopagite systematically worked out for the first time the problem of the nature of God and of our human understanding of it. Dionysius' conception of the 'superessential Godhead' was a Christian idea of God which came very close to the Vedanta. He arrived at a concept of the Godhead that was beyond all name and form; all being, conception or expression. Yet since it was the source of everything that existed, all matter, life, consciousness, reason and will, these things must somehow exist within it, though in a way which transcended conception. Dionysius thus concluded that if man wished to attain to the knowledge of the supreme Godhead, he could only do so by a kind of 'unknowing'; he must pass beyond images and concepts into the darkness of an 'unknowing' which exceeded all knowing. With Dionysius Christian thought, like Hindu thought, had arrived at the idea of the divine being as a hidden mystery, transcending thought, which could only be known by a power beyond reason, which gave a knowledge transcending all knowledge in an actual experience of the divine.

Furthermore, Christian tradition like Hindu tradition recognized that though the divine nature could not properly be known or expressed, there were nonetheless certain terms which could be used particularly appropriately to intimate its nature by analogy. One of these was Being. The name of God as revealed to Moses in the Old Testament was Yahweh, which derived from the root of the verb 'to be'. St Thomas Aquinas, for whom Father Bede had long held a special regard, claimed that Being was the most proper name for God, because it was the least determined of all terms. There was substantial support in Christian tradition for the idea that God was Being itself, not a particular being but the universal ground of all being; not determined by time and space and therefore infinite and eternal; absolutely simple, absolutely full, absolutely unchanging, because it lacked nothing and had nothing to acquire. St John Damascene declared that God was 'an infinite ocean of being'. Father Bede saw the Christian tradition as joining the Hindu tradition in the recognition of God as 'an ocean of being without duality', since to say that the divine being was pure existence without any limitation or qualification was to say that it was absolutely simple and 'without duality'.

To claim that God was Being itself, however, was also to claim that God was consciousness for to lack consciousness was to be deficient in being; it was an imperfect mode of existence. Father Bede was able to go on to establish a relationship between the experience of the Atman in Hindu tradition and the Christian Logos. Consciousness was the reflection of being on itself, but in man this reflection was always imperfect. By reflection on himself, on his thought and his action, he came to know himself but never normally attained to a perfect intuition of himself. Yet it was to this intuition of himself that he constantly aspired and here Hindu thought seemed to Father Bede to mark the greatest insight of the human spirit, for the Hindu sage had always claimed to have reached this intuition of the Self. The experience of the Atman was the soul's direct intuition of itself, in which subject and object were no longer distinguished: the knower, the thing known and the act of knowing were all one. The soul went beyond itself, beyond its phenomenal being and reached the transcendent Self in the consciousness of infinite, transcendent Being. This aspect of the divine nature as transcendent consciousness was known in the Christian tradition as the Logos. The Logos was the principle of all creation, of everything that existed; it was the principle of reason and intelligence, that is of consciousness, in man; and finally it was the principle of self-consciousness in God. Father Bede demonstrated how the Christian faith had arrived at the idea of the Logos as a 'reflection' of God, 'the effulgence of the glory of God and the very image of his being' (Heb. 1.3), a mirror in which the divine being beheld itself. In the Logos or Word the Supreme Being knew itself in an act of reflection on itself. Whereas in the human mind such reflection was normally imperfect, in God there was a perfect reflection of Being on itself. God knew himself in a perfect likeness of himself which was the very expression of his Being. In man the word expressed something of himself – the great poet mirrored himself in his poetry but in God the Word expressed the whole being of God; the Word was a full and perfect expression of God and this was the full and perfect intimacy of self-knowledge for which man craved. The claim of the Hindu seers was that they had had an actual experience of the divine consciousness; this was the very essence of the experience of *saccidananda*. Similarly, in the Christian tradition the saint through his 'participation in the divine nature' (2 Pet. 1.4) came to share in the divine wisdom and knowledge.

On the question of divine consciousness, there were differences within Hinduism itself, between Sankara, Ramanuja and Madhva. All that Father Bede sought to do was to place the Christian experience beside that of the great doctors of the Vedanta and compare them with one another. When it came to the last aspect of the Godhead, that of bliss (*ananda*), he suggested that as there was in human nature a capacity for knowledge, for 'receiving the forms of things into itself, so that the world becomes present to us and we become present to ourselves' so there was a corresponding capacity for love, or self-communication, by which man sought to give himself to others. If then God was infinite Being in perfect consciousness of itself, so then it could be conceived by analogy that in him there was also a delight in being, a pure joy of being, by which in knowing himself he rejoiced in himself. This was the meaning of *ananda*, the pure joy of conscious existence. More than this, however, if there was in God the capacity for self-knowledge, there was also the capacity for self-communication. Father Bede regarded it as one of the important achievements of Vedanta that it had been able to receive into itself the current of *bhakti* or devotion to a personal God and so to conceive of God as love. This was found first of all in the *Bhagavad Gita* but had a long history of development among the Vaishnavite and Saivite devotees. It could not be denied, however, that there had always been a certain conflict in the Hindu tradition between the concept of a personal God who manifested himself in love and the *advaitic* conception of the Brahman as the pure bliss of conscious existence without relationship to another. In Christian tradition the aspect of the Godhead as bliss was represented by the Holy Spirit. As there was in God a Word, by which he knew himself and all things, so there was in him a Spirit by which he communicated himself. There was in God a pure will of love, a pure act of self-giving by which he ceaselessly communicated himself:

> As the Father knows himself in the Son, and the Son in the Father, so Father and Son communicate in the love of the Holy Spirit. The Holy Spirit is this expression of love within the Godhead, the relation of love which unites the persons of the Godhead, and yet there is in it no 'duality' but an identity of nature and consciousness in the bliss of love. Thus the bliss of the Godhead in the Christian view is the overflowing love of God, the mysterious communication of love within the Godhead.

According to Christian faith Jesus Christ was a human being who experienced the mystery of the divine consciousness in a unique way. He knew himself in relation to God as Son of the Father, that is he knew himself to be one with God and yet distinct from him, in an identity of nature but distinction of person. He also experienced the divine love as a gift of the Spirit, a self-communication by which the Father eternally gave himself to him and which he in turn was able to communicate to his disciples. It was from this experience of the mystery of knowledge and love in the Godhead that the Christian doctrine of the Trinity was evolved.

Vedanta and Christian Faith was a very tangible demonstration of how, as Father Bede had advocated some years earlier in *Christian Ashram*, by looking at the Vedanta in depth it was possible for Christians to recover the inner depths of their own religion. The same principle could be applied to a consideration of Christian tradition by Hindus and it was in particular on the question of the nature of the universe and its relation to the ultimate reality that Father Bede continued to think that a comparison with Christian doctrine could be most revealing. Among the points which needed to be further studied was the relationship between the various systems of the Vedanta and the Christian faith on the matter of creation, and, linked to it, the attitude of the Hindu to the external world. In *Vedanta and Christian Faith* Father Bede made a point of stressing that Indian philosophy had never been without a realist element. In all of the three main schools, *Advaita*, *Vishishtadvaita* and *Dvaita*, of which the last might appear the most realist, there was, in Father Bede's view, a firm basis of realism – even in the *Advaita* school of Sankara, the doctrine most commonly accepted by Hindus today and one which at first sight presents the greatest challenge to the realist mind. Since *Christian Ashram* Father Bede had examined more deeply Sankara's assertion that the world of multiplicity was a 'superimposition' on the Absolute Being, that it was like a conjuror's show or a dream which vanished on awakening, that it was an illusion that had no more reality than the form of a snake 'superimposed' on a rope. At a much more profound level Sankara's doctrine was, he felt, based on the great affirmation of the *Upanishads*: 'all this (world) is Brahman' – 'Thou art That'. Sankara had not been denying the reality of this world or of the human subject; he had been denying the ultimate reality of the appearance of this world and of the human person. The objective world was real and the human subject was real but their reality was not what it appeared. Therefore the human mind could not rest on any image presented to the senses or on any thought presented to consciousness. It had to go beyond both image and thought, if it wished to reach the ultimate reality.

In a lecture given in 1974 Father Bede tackled more comprehensively the question of the basic attitude to the 'world' in Asian religions and how far such an attitude was compatible with a Christian view. As so often he confined his attention very largely to the Hindu tradition but it was his belief that the same basic attitudes would be found in

Buddhism and in other Asian religions. In the time of the Vedas (from at least 1500 BC) the prevailing attitude had been one of joyful acceptance of the world in all its beauty and goodness until in the *Upanishads* (about the sixth century BC) the discovery of the transcendent mystery of the Brahman as the Reality underlying all the appearances of the world, and of the Atman, as the ultimate ground of human consciousness beyond sense and thought, had led to a comparative depreciation of the external world and a constant striving to reach beyond sense and thought to the ultimate Reality, beyond time and space. Doubtless, too, the rise of Buddhism with its insistence on the transitory nature of the world and the need to free oneself from all attachment to it and discover the peace of Nirvana, had had a profound effect on Hinduism. The idea of this world as *samsara*, a constant round of births and deaths with no final meaning, and of *moksha* or deliverance from this world as the final goal of life, had become the prevailing attitude of Hinduism no less than Buddhism. Yet in both Father Bede was able to discern a positive acceptance of the world which acted as a counterpoise. The insistence in the *Upanishads* that 'all this world is Brahman' on which Sankara's doctrine was based, the idea that all this world was somehow included in the Brahman, was present at the same time as the constant insistence on the absolute transcendence of the Brahman and the need to turn inwards and discover the Self within. There was in fact no suggestion that the world was unreal but rather that the whole reality of the world came from the Brahman or Atman and was to be referred to it, so that nothing had any real being apart from the Brahman.

The description of the world as *maya* when it first appeared in the *Svetasvatara Upanishad* (about 300 BC) did not carry the meaning of illusion. Much later (in the eighth century AD) according to Sankara the world was *maya* in the sense that it was an 'appearance' of God which was 'inexpressible in terms of being as of not-being'. The world was neither totally real nor totally unreal, and Father Bede was of the opinion that this could be taken in the sense that the world had a certain relative reality, which would bring it near to the Christian idea of creation. The tendency of Sankara to insist that all multiplicity was a 'superimposition' on the One Reality of the Brahman had meant that his doctrine had developed into a form of subjective idealism, which held that the Brahman was pure consciousness and that the world was no more than a false superimposition by the mind of unreal forms on the pure being of the Brahman. This kind of *advaitic* doctrine propagated by Swami Vivekananda in the West had generated the view that Hinduism was a religion in which the world was regarded as unreal, so that not only the material world but also the soul and God had no ultimate reality. The only Reality was the Brahman, which was pure being, consciousness and bliss without any kind of differentiation. There were, however, others who felt, like Father Bede, that this was a misrepresentation of Sankara's thought, and in any case Sankara's was only one school of Hindu thought.

Ramanuja had maintained that the supreme Reality was the personal God (Isvara) and that the world and souls stood to him in the relation of body to soul. God was the inner Ruler, dwelling in the heart of every man, and the destiny of man was not to disappear into the impersonal Godhead, but to be united in love with this supreme Person for all eternity. In the thirteenth century Madhva had gone even further in recognizing the full reality of the world and souls as distinct from God and yet totally dependent on God. Yet in him also the world and souls existed eternally with God in dependence on him but not precisely created by him so that the absolute transcendence of God was not fully realized. It was in the doctrine of Southern Shaivism formulated in the same century after Christ that Father Bede identified a system of belief which came nearest to the Christian. In Shaiva Siddhanta the world and souls existed eternally but God (Shiva) was wholly transcendent and raised man to union with himself by communicating his own divine nature to him. There was no proper place for the body in the state of final bliss, though Father Bede noted that in certain developments of modern Shaivism there was a tendency to believe in the transfiguration of the body by divine grace, but there was a profound realism in this doctrine in which the reality of the world in all its diversity was fully accepted and human life was seen as a deliverance by the grace of God from sin and ignorance, and a communion with God in love.

For Father Bede there could be no doubt that popular Hinduism was largely realistic in its understanding of the world. It was significant also that in the Shastras (the ancient law-books) the four ends of life were said to be not only *moksha* or final deliverance, but also *artha*, wealth, *kama*, pleasure, and *dharma*, duty. Thus a realistic attitude to life had been cultivated from the very beginning. In the *Bhagavad Gita* Krishna advised Arjuna that he must fight in the war to which duty had called him; and the whole purpose of the *Gita* was to proclaim that salvation was to be found not only in the ascetic life of silence and solitude but also in the householder's life of attention to duty. It was this doctrine which Mahatma Gandhi had made the basis of his own life in his struggle to obtain independence for India, and even Vivekananda who had preached the *advaitic* doctrine of Sankara, had nevertheless managed to reconcile it with a powerful advocacy of social reform based on the ideals of the *Bhagavad Gita*. If Father Bede had in the past been prepared to argue that greater concern for one's fellow man was something which Christianity could bring to Hinduism, he was equally prepared to argue that on the basis of the Gita and kindred doctrines, from within Hinduism itself, in modern India the ideals of political action, social service and economic progress had all come to be accepted as legitimate goals. Even Yoga, which Father Bede acknowledged had held in the fourth century the purpose of separating *purusha*, the spirit or consciousness, from its attachment to nature or matter (*prakriti*) so that the soul realized its pure spirituality in isolation (*kaivalya*), had, he asserted, been gradually modified in the light of the Vedanta and under the influence of the *Tantras* (from the sixth century AD). Whereas the Vedanta had always tended to exalt the spirit and depreciate the body, the *Tantras* had proclaimed that it was through the body that the liberation of the spirit was to be attained. The

Tantras were really a sacramental system, by which external rites – *mantras* (sacred words), *mudras* (sacred gestures) and *yantras* (sacred designs) – were used as methods of meditation so as to bring the whole being into union with the divine. Kundalini Yoga was a famous example of precisely this method. Indeed Yoga in the modern world had become a method for the integration of the whole man, body, soul and spirit, with the divine Spirit. Through the practice of *asana* (bodily posture) and *pranayama* (breath-control) the body was brought into a state of harmony, so that all its powers were balanced and integrated. Then the mind was brought under control through *pratyahara* (recollection), *dharana* (concentration) and *dhyana* (meditation, the even flow of concentration), until it eventually became absorbed in the object of contemplation in *samadhi*. There were those who used Yoga as a method of meditation by which the soul was withdrawn from the body and entered into a state of trance; but there were others, and Father Bede was among their number, who conceived of it as a method of integration by which all the faculties of the soul were drawn into the inner centre and gathered into union with the divine Spirit. The most commonly held conception of the perfect state was now one in which the soul enjoyed perfect union with the divine Spirit, but was at the same time able to exercise all its bodily and mental faculties as a *jivan mukto*, one who was 'released' even in this life. In Buddhism there was a similar conception: the highest stage had been reached when *samsara* and *Nirvana* were seen to be the same, when, to express it in Christian terms, the world was seen in God and God in the world.

At the end of his 1974 lecture Father Bede was able to conclude that in general there was no fundamental difference between the Hindu, the Buddhist and the Christian attitude to the world: 'all alike have an other-worldly tendency but all alike have a more realistic attitude in which an equilibrium is found'. The question of the relationship between the world and the sense of the transcendent dimension of existence which may be said to have concerned him since he had first perceived a mysterious presence behind the beauty of nature and first identified the modern western world as ugly because it had lost touch with its roots in feeling and instinct continued to preoccupy Father Bede in a very personal way. The attempt at 'equilibrium' had found its most evident and concrete expression in the Benedictine life of '*ora et labora*', in Father Bede's own acceptance of manual labour as a 'good outlet', and in the social concerns and activities of the ashram which must remain nonetheless a place of prayer where people could find God, where they could experience the reality of the presence of God in their lives and know that they were created not merely for this world but for eternal life.

As a *sannyasi* who had renounced the world, Father Bede was yet sufficiently rooted in his western background and education for him to be unable completely to disregard what science and technology had to offer. It would have been inconceivable that a man of his intellect and vision should fail to take into account the scientific progress which had preoccupied him even as a very young man or to imagine that it could be reversed. What Father Bede did maintain was that the real world was the world as it existed eternally in God. His understanding of evolution was of the gradual ascent of being from the bare potentiality of Aristotle's 'first matter' through the various forms of inorganic being, then of living matter through the various forms of plant and animal, until in man being became conscious of itself. The evolution of man was a gradual ascent through different forms of consciousness, of science, art and morality until he began to realize the divine consciousness which was the ultimate goal in the evolutionary process. Father Bede's idea of the ultimate end of man and the universe was one which could be viewed, as he had shown, as common to both the Hindu and the Christian view: the enjoyment of the divine being, consciousness and bliss. As far as the conception of the end of man was concerned, even the Hindu and Buddhist concept of rebirth could be given a meaning if it was considered that individuals did not exist as isolated units but as members of one body, which was growing throughout human history and was further linked to the evolution of the universe.

Bearing in mind Sankara's saying that 'the Lord is the only transmigrator', Father Bede had some years previously sought to give a meaning to *karma* and transmigration. They had a place not incompatible with Jewish-Christian thought if the body of humanity evolving throughout history was seen as the sphere of the divine action which was gradually leading it out of its fallen state of sin into its ultimate state of blissful participation in the divine life. His concept of the transformation of matter into life and consciousness was based alike on the thought of Sri Aurobindo and Teilhard de Chardin, the idea being that the whole development of the cosmos was implicit in the first explosion of matter. Matter gradually evolved through sub-atomic particles to simple atoms, then molecules and, when the earth was ready for it, living cells, plants, animals and human beings. According to David Bohm's theory of the 'implicate order' all this development was implicit from the beginning. Everything was 'implicated' and then gradually 'explicated' to assume the forms we know.

According to Sri Aurobindo and Teilhard de Chardin mental consciousness in human beings led on to 'supermental' consciousness in the great saints and sages, until they came to divine consciousness, for a Christian in Jesus. This was according to St Paul's theory of the 'recapitulation of all things in Christ' (Eph. 1.10). To Father Bede the whole universe was one body, one organic whole which came to a head in man. There was one Self who became incarnate in humanity. Mankind as a whole, humanity in the total course of its history was the body of this Self, the indwelling Spirit. All men, as Aquinas claimed, (*Summa Theologica* 1a.11ae.81.1) are one Man, and it was this one Man who fell in Adam and was redeemed in Christ. The full meaning of the incarnation was the assumption of the whole universe and the whole of humanity into the divine life. It was this which was revealed in the resurrection. 'The body of Christ', Father Bede would write in *Return to the Centre*, was formed from the matter of the universe, from the actual particles, protons, electrons, neutrons, atoms, molecules, which constitute matter. Just as these particles are organized into living cells and begin to perform the functions of life; and just as the living cells are formed into animal organisms and begin to perform the functions of animal life; and as the animal organism with its atoms and molecules and cells is formed into a human being and begins to exercise rational activity; so in the resurrection these same particles of matter, these living cells, this animal organism, were formed into a 'spiritual body', a body filled with divine life and participating in the divine consciousness.

The inner movement of the Spirit, immanent in nature, which effected the evolution of matter and life into consciousness, and the same Spirit at work in human consciousness, latent in every man, was, according to Father Bede, always at work, leading to divine life. Deep in the depths of any being, a grain of sand, a leaf, a flower was the eternal mystery. Beyond the molecules and atoms, the protons and electrons, beyond the living cell was an energy, a force of life continually welling up from the abyss of being in the Father, continually springing up in the light of the Word, continually flowing back to its source in the bliss of love. At the heart of every creature lay what was best described in terms of the divine *saccidananda*, the Holy Trinity, but which ultimately defied even that description. *Saccidananda*, the 'transcendent Mystery', the 'ultimate Truth', the 'universal Law' were but expressions used to express the inexpressible, to cast but a glimmer of light upon a mystery which continually baffled human reason. All the constructions of mathematical reason on the basis of the senses, all the grandiose systems of philosophy based on sense and reason, were only the reflection in the human mind of a Reality which always transcended it, and so the great illusion, '*maya*' actually consisted in imagining that the construction which our senses put upon this world was the ultimate reality.

One afternoon, in the course of my stay at Saccidananda Ashram, I would walk with Father Bede round the ten acres of land which by that time supported the community. The land within the immediate vicinity was mostly grazing land for a bullock team and for cows which lived a life unsegregated from the continuous flow of humans for whom they provided milk. There was little surplus to be sold in the nearby village, but the community had also planted mango trees and over 200 coconut palms. Each of the last was expected to bear about 100 coconuts which would be sold at one rupee each and contribute to a basic income for the ashram so that it was not too heavily dependent on gifts from outside. The brothers were still living from month to month and trusting in Divine Providence. A legacy from a friend of Father Bede had first enabled them to build, regular gifts from a lady in America had supported them for five years, six years previously the Indian government had given them the use of an acre on which the brothers had been able to build not permanent constructions but mud huts somewhat removed from the increasing number of guests, and so it had continued. Further along the river bank, beyond Marie Louise's ashram, lay a four acre field which the ashram had bought in 1980 with money provided by an American charitable foundation. With the minimum use of artificial fertilizer and the maximum application of natural manure, for organic farming was the real objective, this field provided rich crops of paddy, maize, groundnuts and coconuts. There had been never too much money, never enough to allow extravagance and never really too little. It was Father Bede's hope that this would never change: money was so seductive, so terribly corrupting. Achieving an appropriate level of poverty and simplicity in the life of the ashram was a continuing problem. Father Monchanin's principle had been that there should be nothing in the ashram which the local villagers did not have. Father Bede recognized the validity of certain necessities. When first he had come there had been no electricity. He had subsequently installed an electric pump and eventually a motor pump so that when the current failed a reserve was available. Now electricity was fairly common in the village. So too were televisions and tractors. Father Monchanin's principle was not quite so readily applicable.

There had been a time when the local workers had used tractors to farm the ashram land but Father Bede was still ill at ease with machinery. At Prinknash he had come to recognize that even mechanical work could be made a genuine sacrifice, an offering to God. He had realized also that machinery had its value not only in relieving human drudgery but as an instrument of producing better work. There was beauty in the products of the machine, in the car, the ship or the aeroplane when used according to the true purposes of nature. The evil of industrialism had been due to the abuse of the machine, to the lust for material wealth and the contempt for the human person. If the machine was used in the service of God and with respect to the fundamental needs of human nature, then it could take its place in society, but so often the machine seemed to be of value only in producing things more quickly or more easily or in greater quantity, and not in making them intrinsically better and therefore more beautiful. Rarely also did the machine give the human workman real satisfaction. In what he considered something of a triumph, Father Bede had succeeded in getting rid of the tractors at Saccidananda Ashram and the noise that came with them, and restoring the use of bullock carts and traditional Indian ploughs, except in the event of an emergency.

In silence we passed the great banyan tree with a palm growing up through its middle, in a hollow of which Abhishiktananda used to sit and meditate. Beyond the ashram gates we walked through the woodland that fringed the Cauvery to be greeted with a chorus of 'hellos' from a group of workers returning from their labours in the fields and collecting brushwood for their fires. The ashram employed a dozen workers on a permanent basis but at harvest time or on other similar occasions as many as fifty labourers were collected from the village. To each of the more permanent workers the ashram had given a small plot of land so that they would always have some means of providing for their families. The ashram's simplicity, the concern, the hospitality, the cultivation – it was all part of a positive acceptance of the world, and even in the heart of rural India, in the old 'sacral' universe where amongst the palmyra palms, the eucalyptus trees and the huge exotic blooms many customs had not changed for centuries, such an acceptance meant coming to grips with the currents of the modern world. Some distance upstream from the ashram contemporary technology had built a gigantic dam across the sacred river. Its waters were now distributed over a wider area and the ashram and lands that bordered on the Cauvery were no longer threatened by annual flooding. Yet even this great dam was not an unmixed blessing. In the dry months now the mile wide river was reduced to several thin streams which trickled their way falteringly through the vast expanse of sand. In these murky runnels the local people bathed and washed their clothes and from them came the water for drinking, and for the cattle and the crops. That they resented the diversion of the previously abundant flow could hardly be surprising. There was good and evil latent in all progress.

By the time he wrote *Return to the Centre* Father Bede had come to view modern science and technology as the fruit of the tree of the knowledge of good and evil. They were not evil in themselves but they became evil when, as so often happened, they were separated, not now as he might once have put it, from feeling and instinct but from wisdom; and wisdom consisted in awakening to the deep truth of Sankara's *Advaita*, to the knowledge that when considered apart from Brahman this world had no reality at all. Paradoxically, once this was realized, by the same mysterious process that determined that the man who laid down his life would find it, the world recovered its reality, but it was a reality which could not be grasped by reason alone. In Father Bede's scale of values science was the lowest form of human knowledge – the knowledge of the material world through discursive reason. Philosophy, though still confined to discursive reason, ranked higher because it went beyond the material world to explore the world of thought. Theology came above philosophy because it was open to the world of transcendent reality but its methods were still those of science and philosophy. Only wisdom could transcend reason and know the Truth, not discursively but intuitively, not by its reflection in the world of the senses but in its Ground, where knowing was also being. Separated from wisdom every advance in science brought a corresponding evil in its train. Reason subject to the eternal Law, the universal Reason, became Wisdom. It knew the Self. Otherwise it could seek to be master of the world and then it became demonic. Reason was the demon of the modern world. It was also the serpent instrumental in man's Fall. In every generation the Fall of Man was repeated: the fall from the being, consciousness and bliss of eternal existence in the Word, the fall from that point at which the Atman was one with the Brahman, from the Centre of freedom and immortality, into subjection to the senses and imprisonment in the material world in which the vision of eternity and the hope of immortality was lost. Never perhaps had the Fall of Man been repeated on a wider scale than today.

Although Father Bede was by no means unaware of the growing impact of science and technology upon India itself, *Return to the Centre* was addressed very much to a western readership. Its message was essentially that the true Centre of man's being was not the ego which sought to make itself independent and master the world but the 'I' beyond this, a deeper Centre of personal Being which was grounded in the Truth and which was one with the universal Self, the Law of the Universe. This was the great discovery of Indian thought, but it was something that had been implicitly recognized by every ancient culture. The focal point of all such cultures, whether in the form of a place, a building or a person had always been a point where contact could be made with the source of being, a point where heaven and earth converged, where human life was open to the Transcendent. The modern world was removing such points of contact. For so many today sex was the one means of opening to the divine, to the world of transcendent mystery, but sex was but the shadow of love and had therefore always to be transcended. The young people who came to India from the West were rebelling against a profane and one-dimensional life and seeking to recover the sense of the sacred which India too was in danger of losing. The essential need in the modern world was to recover the sense of the transcendent Reality and the road to such a recovery lay not via modern science which failed to take into account the fact that the material world was a part – an inferior part – of a greater whole, and which ignored the legacy of ancient tradition that recognized three 'worlds' – the physical, the psychic and the spiritual – interdependent as an integrated whole. Nor did it lie via the path of a discursive reason which insisted upon the exclusive reality of the world of the senses. Rather it lay via a return to the wisdom of the unconscious, to the heart of the child that was hidden in every man. It called for a readiness to learn from every ancient tradition and for a revival of man's sense of solidarity with nature, nature not seen as an external object to be studied by cold reason but as a living part of man's being. It called for a vision of an integral science, one such as Goethe had envisaged, a science in which the laws of matter were studied in relation to the psychic laws on which they depended, and these in turn to the ultimate spiritual law. It called also for the recognition that the world as seen by a poet, by a Dante, a Chaucer or a Shakespeare, was more, not less real than the world seen by the ordinary man; that the poet, the painter and the artist were in touch with the transcendent Mystery; that the sphere of myth opened the mind to a higher state of consciousness than that of 'facts' and that the experience of the mystic in the ground of the soul, though beyond words or sounds or images, was yet of infinite value.

Return to the Centre was manifestly the work of a man of learning and intellect but it read more like a series of meditations inviting intuitive understanding than an intellectual thesis. Could it be that Father Bede's own life reflected the very *metanoia* he was advocating – the passage from rational knowledge to intuitive wisdom? What better exponent of the limitations of the intellectual faculty could there be than one who had used that very faculty so effectively throughout his life and who yet knew from personal experience of the need to surrender reason and the individual Self to the great Self, the universal, cosmic consciousness? Long ago in Bethnal Green Father Bede had recognized that his mistake had been to make himself the centre of his own existence, that his isolation from the rest of the world was due to the fact that he had deliberately shut himself up within the barriers of his own will and reason, and that he was being called upon to surrender that independence. As once he had written of the need to surrender to the love of God, of how the end of the golden string had been offered to him not as a result of all his study or of any act of his own will, so now he was writing of how the Self, the Truth, the inner Centre of being, could not be reached by any human effort, not by science, philosophy, technology, social engineering or by any technique for it was not the mind which grasped the Self, but the Self which grasped the mind. The path of wisdom, of return to the Self or Centre was that intimated by the *Katha Upanishad* 3.13: 'The wise should surrender speech in mind, mind in the knowing Self, the knowing Self in the great Self, the great Self in the Self of peace.' Perhaps then there was a reflection of personal experience also in his expressed conviction that when reason surrendered to the Self it lost none of its powers. The mind of a Sankara or an Aquinas was equal to that of any modern scientist or philosopher, but it drew on sources of wisdom which raised it to a higher power and carried it beyond their reach. Reason surrendered to the Self rose to the peak of its ability.

Time and again Father Bede would return to the importance of maintaining before society the goal of transcendence, without which secular living lost its meaning. In this task the monk had a significant role. Yet the contemporary world had stopped at the second *ashrama*. It had no place for the *vanaprastha* and the *sannyasi*, no place for the monk. The contemporary world recognized three of the four 'ends' of life of ancient India but not the last, *moksha*, liberation, the final goal of ultimate transcendence. It had a place for three of ancient India's original four castes but not for the Brahmin or priest. Yet it was the priest who kept the link with the ultimate meaning of life. Inevitably the failure of society to accord to the transcendent its proper place represented a challenge to the Church, but what was the Church? The Church was the Body of Christ, the visible structure in which the mystery of the divine life among men was being manifested. It was not possible to conceive this Church in isolation from the rest of the world. From the beginning of history this Body of Christ which was the body of humanity had been growing age by age. Every religion had contributed to the building of this temple, every human being was a member of this Body.

The man whom Lewis had once accused of concentrating on the divisions that existed between the various religions was able now to argue that the divine Mystery was present everywhere in the hearts of all men and in every religion, and the fact that he could do so was a vindication of his early assertion that the path of reconciliation would not be found by ignoring such differences but by studying them at their deepest level. By doing precisely that he had come to the understanding that we come forth from the One and are returning to the One, that the essential message of all religion was the divine life among men, that every religious doctrine always ended in mystery and that the Truth was found beyond all the formulations of the schools and beyond all the revelations of the scriptures in the inner depths of the heart, beyond words and thought, where the divine Word was spoken and the mystery of Being was made known. The essential truth could not be put into words. It was known only in the silence, in the stillness of the faculties. As Meister Eckhart had put it, 'There is nothing so much like God as silence.' Thus all external religion, with its rites and dogma and organization existed only to lead men to the knowledge of the inner mystery. Now that no religion could remain in isolation the way forward was through a critical evaluation of all by which the limitations of historical conditions could be discerned and the essential Truth, which was ultimately One, discovered. The real challenge to the Christian Church was now that the structure of doctrine and ritual and organization which it had inherited were no longer adequate to express the divine Mystery. When the dogmas of the Church, instead of opening the heart and mind to the mystery of love, became obstacles to the knowledge of the Truth, it was obvious that they had ceased to serve their purpose. Yet the solution was not the abolition of the Church, of dogma, ritual and organization which ultimately would result in another Church, another dogma, another ritual and another form of organization. Rather, every religion had continually to evolve and to renew itself.

It was no doubt in this light that Father Bede's views on the papacy as expressed some years later when Pope John Paul II's proposed visit to Britain had been announced, were to be considered. The present system of the papacy, which he felt most people would agree was the greatest obstacle to reunion of the Christian Churches, was not something that belonged to the permanent constitution of the Church. It had grown up in the Middle Ages in the West and its structure had been determined by historical circumstances which were no longer valid today. Father Bede advocated renewal which would involve gradually, with the tide of ecumenism, moving out of the very limited structure of the existing Catholic Church but it was a form of renewal which also represented a return. The 'blueprint' which Father Bede offered for an ecumenical and decentralized Church in which the papacy would be a centre of unity rather than of control took as its model the structure of the Church in the fifth century, which, while recognizing the primacy of the Bishop of Rome as the successor of St Peter also held in no less honour four other 'patriarchates'. Since the Second Vatican Council the different bishops' conferences had gradually begun to assume an authority over their respective Churches and it would not, argued Father Bede, be difficult to envisage a development of these conferences into something like the ancient patriarchates. Each of the five proposed conferences – of Europe, of North America, of South America, of Africa and of Asia together with Australia – would be, like the ancient patriarchates, responsible for their Churches in every way, with their own liturgy, system of theology and ecclesiastical organization. Historically the

Pope had never normally interfered in the affairs of another patriarchate except when a dispute arose which could not otherwise be settled. Such an arrangement would allow scope for development of doctrine and liturgy in the context of different cultures. If the Orthodox and the Anglican Churches were to be reunited, they would each form a separate bishops' conference, managing their own affairs in all things, only acknowledging a centre of unity in the Church of Rome and a right of recourse in matters of dispute. Other Christian Churches, which were prepared to recognize this ministry in the service of unity in the Bishop of Rome, would also be able to form lesser conferences in communion with the larger ones.

This would demand a recognition of other forms of ministry in the Church beside the traditional ones of bishop, priest and deacon. It would demand the acceptance of married clergy and would allow for the ordination of women to the ministry on a basis of equality with men. In the light of the Second Vatican Council the doctrine of papal infallibility could be given a new interpretation. The Council had made it possible to see that the Pope had no authority apart from the laity, the people of God. The gift of infallibility was given by Jesus to the whole Church when he communicated to the Church the gift of the Holy Spirit, which was to guide his disciples into all truth. This gift of the Spirit was given to all Christians at their baptism and every Christian shared in the teaching authority of the Church. The bishops and the Pope had a special ministry of service to the Church in preserving the truth of the apostolic teaching, but this authority could only be exercised in so far as they shared in the communion of all the faithful. The charism of infallibility, or more simply, of adherence to the truth of the Gospel, therefore, belonged to the whole Church, though it could be exercised on occasion by the Pope or the bishops, in the name of the Church.

Father Bede's 'blueprint' was offered in *The Tablet* as something to be considered, discussed and, if necessary, 'to be changed out of all recognition'. Even so by his own admission, it had taken courage to write and it would be some time before he would muster the nerve to further pursue his vision of a Church which preserved a tradition but to which everyone could come, a Church which was always open to the movement of history and the people.

When, in February 1986, Pope John Paul II visited India he stressed two main themes. In his first speech, in Delhi, to the assembled bishops of India, he spoke of the challenge of 'inculturation', of the need to express Christian faith and worship in a language and liturgy that reflected local culture. The second theme which the Pope emphasized was the need for dialogue. Both themes Father Bede welcomed with enthusiasm. It could hardly escape a less involved observer, however, that some thirty-six years had elapsed since Fathers Monchanin and Le Saux had made their first step in the direction of bridging the gulf between the Christian culture in India and the Indian culture proper, and even Father Bede was compelled to acknowledge that progress had been slow. The beginnings of an Indian liturgy had been approved by the bishops and the Holy See but its use was still limited. Despite the attempt to create an Indian theology expressing the Christian faith not in terms of Greek or European philosophy but in terms of Vedanta, Indian theology was still more concerned with liberation and too strongly influenced by the Latin American model. As far as dialogue was concerned considerable progress had been made. Meetings were taking place between Hindus, Muslims and Christians for theological discussion as well as for joint prayer and social action. Nevertheless all these developments were confined to a minority. The Church as a whole remained fixed in its old traditions. Father Bede was still having to press home his message of the need for a Church for the world.

With regard to the quest for an integral science there were perhaps greater grounds for optimism. In 1982 in Bombay, at a conference organized by the Californian Institute of Transpersonal Psychology on western science and eastern wisdom Father Bede came into direct contact with Dr Fritjof

Capra. Dr Capra was the author of *The Tao of Physics* in which he had shown that the New Physics as it was now understood had a vision of the universe very close to the vision of ancient Indian and Chinese thought and very different from that which had prevailed in the West during the last two or three centuries. Humanity was really emerging into a new vision of reality, a new paradigm. In *The Turning Point* he had gone on also to apply the new paradigm not only to physics, but also to biology, psychology, sociology, medicine and economics. A totally new vision was emerging. After the splitting of the atom and the resultant discovery that matter no longer obeyed the laws of Isaac Newton there had followed the Quantum Theory of Heisenberg, Bohr and others in the 1920s. It was discovered that matter was not the solid substance hitherto imagined; its texture was not solid at all. A microscope revealed, below the atom, electrons, protons and neutrons. A hundred such particles were discovered and all these particles were constantly vibrating. Furthermore it was discovered that below the sub-atomic level it was impossible to tell whether the object observed was a particle or a wave. Under certain conditions the object appeared to be a particle, under others a wave. Science had come round to the view now universally accepted that matter was not an extended substance but energy. Humankind was living in a field of energy which was in constant flux, constant change. Dr Capra described it as 'a complicated web of inter-dependent relationships'. Hitherto it had been believed that by getting down to the parts, the atoms, it would be possible to explain the whole, but in the new system of understanding the parts were all integrated as elements in the whole and no part of the universe could be understood except in relation to the whole. In a sense the whole was present in every part. This, together with David Bohm's theory of the 'implicate order', reflected a changed vision of reality and one which in seeing the world as a field of energy in which everything was in constant interplay with everything else was almost exactly the Buddhist view of the universe.

Similarly in the field of biology the mechanistic system by

which life was explained in terms of physics and chemistry and the theory of chance and necessity was seen to be collapsing. During a stay at Saccidananda Ashram, the biologist Rupert Sheldrake, a personal friend of Father Bede, wrote his book *A New Science of Life* introducing the concept of what he called 'morphogenetic fields', fields which were responsible for producing form. Despite all the great achievements of molecular biology, it could not explain the phenomena of life. The incredible subtlety, beauty and complexity of natural life in the universe could not be adequately accounted for in terms of chance and natural selection and Sheldrake maintained that there must be some power which formed these elements. His idea of morphogenetic fields was of a structure of energy which gave form to the universe. He was in a sense restoring Aristotle's idea of the Formal Cause, the idea that there must be some structural power in nature apart from mere energy which produced atoms, molecules and cells, organisms and living beings; and once formal causality had been allowed, once it had been acknowledged that there was a structuring power in the universe, then meaning and purpose in the universe was also allowed. Thus the New Science was beginning to see that there was a marvellous power at every level, which organized the elements to produce the varied forms of nature; that there was meaning behind all this and that there was purpose in the whole scheme.

The approach to consciousness had changed also. Descartes had seen mind and consciousness as completely separate from the material universe, but Einstein had broken down this division, by maintaining that the observer affects whatever he is observing. With quantum physics it was found that the mechanisms used to observe the atom and sub-atomic particles affected the behaviour of the atom and its particles. Nature could not be observed as it was; it could only be observed through the senses, through the instruments used and through mental concepts. So Heisenberg, who was both a scientist and a philosopher, was able to state that science did not simply describe and explain nature, it was part of the interplay between nature and man; it was nature observed through the human body and mind. It was not possible to separate what the individual was observing from his consciousness. Nature was matter and life as observed through human consciousness. They were interdependent. Science was beginning to be seen as a symbolic system in recognition of the fact that all that science could give was a symbolic understanding of the universe, one which was very pure, very effective, able to produce marvellous things, but nevertheless a limited symbolic understanding. It could not tell what the reality was. The scientist did not know reality in itself. He only knew reality through the symbols and the signs which made reality present to him but which could never exhaust and manifest reality in its fullness.

So science had its value but it was limited. Beyond the physical scientific universe was the psychological universe, the universe of poetry, music, dance and all the human relationships expressed through words, gestures and language. There were those who were beginning to see that the psychological world was not simply subjective but was more real than the physical world. The psychologist Ken Wilber, author of *The Spectrum of Consciousness*, *Up from Eden* and *The Atman Project*, was urging the necessity to make use of western psychology which had provided so many valuable insights but also expounding the need to progress beyond it. Educated in the tradition of Freud and Jung he went beyond western psychology into Vedanta, Mahayana Buddhism and Taoism. In America the realm of Transpersonal Psychology, of Para-psychology, of the realm of consciousness beyond the ego, beyond the mental self was being explored. Para-psychology included phenomena such as telepathy, telekinesis, clairvoyance and healing, now considered worthy subjects for study.

This sphere beyond the mental consciousness Father Bede called the psychic. To him there was a physical world and the ordinary psychological world, and there was the psychic world which was just as real as the external phenomena he observed. He knew, and science had confirmed his knowledge, that external phenomena were not as they appeared at all. He was not a solid body and the material universe was not a solid body, as it appeared. Para-psychology dealt with phenomena which were no less real than material phenomena. He had sat beside Premananda during his visit to the ashram from Sri Lanka, and he had seen him produce, as if from the atmosphere, sandal powder which the Swami had poured into Father Bede's hand. Such phenomena were real but they were still not beyond phenomena. Wilber, the psychologist, maintained that the whole movement of the human race and the whole universe was towards the Ultimate Reality, the Atman, the supreme reality which was beyond all phenomena. Western science and psychology in general were waking up to the fact that there was something beyond all phenomena, and Father Bede, who even as a very young man had pursued his conception of imagination as the power to see beyond the phenomenon and grasp the reality which underlay this world's appearances, was convinced that mankind should not stop at any phenomena whatsoever. The vision of the early *Upanishadic* tradition was of going beyond all phenomena to the transcendent Self. This was the vision that the western world had since lost and this was the vision that must be restored. How far that process of restoration was already underway was perhaps immeasurable, as immeasurable as the Absolute present in the universe but so frequently unperceived.

13

A Model for the World

Father Bede had been travelling. He had travelled a long way both in mind and in space and time since first he had watched the sun setting over the playing fields of Christ's Hospital. Talking in his thatched hut set among the tall palmyra trees beneath the same sun but one which could so easily be taken for larger, fiercer, different, he expressed the fear that his life must seem rather dull since so much of it had been spent in monasteries, 'but of course a good deal goes on under the surface'. There had come a time too when it had seemed appropriate to travel beyond the boundaries of India. He had returned at intervals to England, had visited his family and the number of nieces and nephews who were 'rather nice people' and who accepted him for what he was, unperturbed by the flowing hair and the saffron robes of a *sannyasi*. The man who had long ago been afraid to spend a whole night in prayer for fear of what people might think, had made a point of wearing *kavi* even when journeying in Europe. He would not be happy in anything else: it was a sign which set him apart but which, because it was not clerical in any way, did not make him unapproachable. He had visited his friends of so many years Martyn Skinner and, until his death, Hugh Waterman. When writing to them, as he regularly did, he seemed to see himself as he was when he was about twenty and thought of them as they were then. In England he found them physically changed but otherwise little altered. They still argued over the things which had always provoked differences of opinion. As for Martyn Skinner, he teased his friend about his travels – 'If you want to see the world become a monk' – and preserved a certain ambivalence in his attitude towards Father Bede's flying. Father Bede's motive, the need to spread the gospel, was doubtless the best, but Martyn Skinner was not entirely sure that the ends justified the means. Nor did he think that flying suited him. On the whole, however, he was full of admiration for the fact that, apart from the occasional use of airports and planes, 'old Bede' was the only one of the three who had remained true to their original vision. One episode during one of Father Bede's stays would remain vivid in his memory. Father Bede had been standing on the lawn looking rather like St Peter when suddenly Cristudas, who had accompanied him on that occasion, swept up a strawberry net that had been drying on the grass and wrapped it round and round him. Father Bede passively endured his captivity in a rather comic manner, which provoked from his friend the comment: 'You can't imagine St Andrew doing that to St Peter, not because they were apostles, but because they were fishermen.'

There had been visits to Prinknash, during which his fellow monks claimed to see little of him because he was in such great demand elsewhere. Father Bede gave talks and lectures and cemented relationships throughout the world. He led people in meditation; for meditation, in taking individuals beyond the senses and beyond the mind, brought them to experience something of the transcendent reality, and as that experience grew affected their whole attitude to the world around them. He was written about in the press, in German, French, Italian and a multitude of other languages. He celebrated Mass in the Indian rite in Abingdon, in America, in Australia where it was shown on television, in numerous places scattered across the continents, for the word was spreading. In 1985 he would attend a meeting in Madras on the theme of 'Emerging Consciousness for a New Humankind' inaugurated by the Dalai Lama whom Father Bede then and over tea afterwards found to be 'a very beautiful and open person of tremendous compassion and understanding'. The conference brought together representatives of all the main religions of Asia. This and many other gatherings reflected the fact that in many parts of the world and among very different people it was felt that a new consciousness was emerging which could change man's understanding of reality. For Father Bede the venture into the new, his vision of how the Christian faith could be lived in the oriental tradition supported by modern western scientific understanding, had ceased to be so predominantly a struggle. He had discovered himself in harmony with a gathering movement around him. Increasingly he found himself carried by the tide and not simply fighting against it.

In 1978 Father Bede had been invited to celebrate Mission Sunday in Milan. The talk and meditation he gave there was attended by 100,000 people. In the following year, together with Amaldas, in the space of two months he visited monasteries in fifteen different American States, again giving talks and leading meditations. There was, however, another reason for so comprehensive a tour. The growing inter-national interest had brought home to the community in Saccidananda Ashram the need to clarify its status. The period during which Father Bede had been very much against links with western congregations, to the extent of rejecting even western singing, was over. Contact with other monast-eries provided the opportunity to look into the possibility of becoming affiliated to or oblates of another monastic community. There were many American monasteries who were interested in Father Bede's work. Holy Trinity Abbey in New York were particularly forward looking and the possibility of affiliation seemed feasible but the difficulty of preserving the degree of freedom necessary for the life of the ashram in India was not easily surmounted. Father Bede had maintained a very good relationship with the Benedictines in England. He returned to Prinknash Abbey and the Brothers made him very welcome and understood very well what the small community in Shantivanam was trying to do, but the structure and life of the Benedictines was not for the members of an Indian ashram.

Eventually Father Bede went to Italy and it was in the semi-hermitic, semi-community life of the Camaldoli order that he found something closely approaching the life of the ashram. Camaldoli united solitary life and community life together with great openness to the world. St Romuald, its founder, had further provided for the life of the wandering monk going out to preach the gospel. Not only, therefore, was it possible to find in the Camaldoli life a reflection of the ideal of Hindu monasticism which had always favoured both the solitary life of the hermit in the Himalayas and the community life of the ashram, but also *parivrajya* the life of the wandering monk who journeys from place to place, returning to his ashram in the rainy season. A Camaldoli Brother had already spent a year on the ashram and when he returned to his monastery he shared with his community what he had experienced at Shantivanam. The prior general was able readily to accept the idea of a monastic community in India according to the Indian culture preserving the spirit of Camaldoli with the minimum of rules, and in 1980, after a stay in the monastery in Italy, Father Bede became formally affiliated to Camaldoli.

The situation with regard to Amaldas and Cristudas had been more complex for since completing their novitiate and making their first profession at Kurisumala they had not renewed their vows. Consequently they were strictly speaking lay people and could not join the Camaldoli congregation. With an eye to the future, however, both had some years previously embarked upon studies for the priesthood. They had recognized that the community could not afford to depend for its future upon the readiness of a priest from outside to celebrate Mass according to the rite used in the ashram. Not so very long after Father Bede had become a Benedictine monk of the Camaldoli congregation, Amaldas and Cristudas made their final profession at Shantivanam in a ceremony attended by the Prior General of the Camaldoli. They then completed their diaconate and six months later were ready for ordination. Meanwhile they had spent some time in the monastery in Italy and at San Gregorio, the Camaldoli house in Rome. They were finally ordained at Saccidananda Ashram in a service for which the great *pandal* that would remain thereafter covering the outer area of the temple was erected. It was a vitally significant occasion.

Priesthood meant involvement in all the structure of the institutional Church and the sacramental system which Father Bede knew could be inhibiting. In a way it was wrong that it should carry with it such prestige but at the same time it would set the ashram on its feet. That night, after evening prayers, Amaldas and Cristudas found Father Bede sitting in his room with tears pouring down his cheeks. It was a display of emotion, the very rarity of which bespoke the depth of feeling that engendered it. He was weeping not in sadness but for joy at the fact that the two young men whom he had welcomed as sons and whom he had watched grow to maturity, not always without pain and conflict, had reached 'a great fulfilment'. In them the ashram had borne fruit and through them its future was more secure.

The formal reception of the ashram into the Camaldolese congregation in 1982 and the ordination of Amaldas and Cristudas in January 1986 gave to the community a new and more clearly defined status, and with 'respectability' came easier acceptance in those quarters where previously there had been opposition. Relations with the local bishop, who had in any case undergone a change of heart, had improved greatly. In Rome too affiliation to the community which had a house in San Gregorio did the ashram in India no harm. The resultant easier atmosphere within the community brought Father Bede, who for all his conviction that he must not seek guarantees even for the present, had undoubtedly been suffering from stress, greater peace of mind. His appetite, often better when during his travels he had the opportunity to eat European food, and his health improved. Marie Louise provided for him a spice free diet of vegetables and fruit and curds, Cristudas massaged him regularly, and Father Bede was able to abandon the medicines he had been taking for his heart. In the temple he allowed himself a cushion to make it possible for him to sit cross-legged for longer periods of time, but otherwise he was as vigorous as ever. Only when overtired or upset or when flying did his irregular heartbeat cause him trouble now.

The jubilee of his entry into the religious life was celebrated at Shantivanam in traditional Indian fashion. Both Father Bede and the cosmic cross in the temple were anointed with water from the sacred River Cauvery. It was an inspiring ceremony, an occasion of great joy, and no doubt of that kind of joy which C.S. Lewis had maintained emphasized man's pilgrim status, the joy that 'reminds, beckons, awakens desire', yet in one sense at least, Father Bede's pilgrimage was nearing its conclusion. By the time we met at Saccidananda Ashram Father Bede had reached a point where he felt that he would no longer travel outside India. It was not so much a concession to his health and his age, although his eightieth birthday was approaching, as the product of the feeling that there was a time in life in which to go out to the world and a time to allow the world to come to you. This feeling was endorsed at a very practical level by the fact that when last he had left India, to visit Australia, he had experienced some difficulty in obtaining a re-entry visa. The Indian Government had always been very good to Father Bede. The Indian character of the ashram had been fully appreciated and until 1984 its Superior had experienced no difficulties. A well-disposed local superintendent of police had approved his passport not as that of a missionary but as that of a *sannyasi* which meant that he had not been subject to the restrictions imposed upon missionaries. With the introduction of the 1984 Bill requiring all Commonwealth citizens to register, however, his position was somewhat changed. He was granted an initial three-month visa but on application for a resident's permit he received no response. He and others in a similar predicament had decided to depend, without exerting undue pressure, upon the reluctance of the Indian government actually to require them to leave.

After so many years in India, years in which the Indian psychology had become so much a part of him, a possible solution might be to apply for Indian citizenship. It was something which he had considered and to which he would be quite open, for a *sannyasi* is beyond all social states. He did not belong anywhere in particular; and if Father Bede did not like the politics of India he was equally unenamoured of Mrs

Thatcher's Britain. He had never felt any nostalgia for England. Moments of loneliness in a land so very different from the country of his origins had been rare, for Amaldas and Cristudas had been with him and there were always the Indian people with whom he experienced that almost physical feeling of oneness. Yet to give up English citizenship would, Father Bede acknowledged, be a 'sort of break'. The whole past was there with him. There was still an attachment to that.

We had spent a number of hours together in his little hut, one small room with a concrete floor and a thatched roof, furnished with a bed, a chair, a table, a typewriter and shelves on which he kept some books and papers, copies of articles he had written, the photocopies of C. S. Lewis' later letters in an old brown envelope. Such simple items were, Father Bede had pointed out apologetically, luxuries for a *sannyasi* but he had never been able to sit or sleep always on the floor. A *sannyasi* renounced all possessions but the key to renunciation was in detachment. What was important was that although he had the use of the books, the typewriter and other basic items they were not really 'his'. It did not matter so much what material possessions a person had, provided he was not attached to them. He had sat upon his wooden chair and I on his bed, and I had listened as Father Bede talked of his life almost as if it were the life of another, something which he could survey with a dispassionate interest and at times with an easy humour that brought a gentle smile to his blue-grey eyes. His inner struggle had left its mark upon his face but now it was as if he had reached the state of one who dwelt in his inner self and was the same in pleasure and in pain. He had made himself as available and as open as he could, and I was conscious of the great trust vested in me. Yet there remained as if in the air between us the feeling that the real substance of his life was something which defied expression. On more than one occasion I had heard him quote from St Thomas Aquinas, author of the supremely logical, rational *Summa Theologica*: 'Everything I have written seems to me like empty straw compared to what I have seen.' I was left with the impression that the witness of Father Bede's life was to a not dissimilar experience.

In the course of my month at Saccidananda Ashram I had watched the steady flow of people come and go. Americans, Australians, New Zealanders, Europeans and Indians – they too were travelling. Some were touring the ashrams of India for no other reason than that they offered cheap accommodation, payment being often, as here, at the discretion of the visitor. Others were evidently exploring the wealth of psychic phenomena that secret India had to offer. Yet others were on a conscious spiritual quest. Lay people and religious of a variety of denominations came there on retreat, and there were those, too, who simply chanced upon the entrance to the ashram. Saccidananda Ashram had its share of drug addicts and the mentally unstable. Visitors to the 'abode of peace' beside the great Ganges of the South formed a microcosm of society and almost irrespective of their motive for wishing to come Father Bede made them welcome. The only condition of their residence was that they attend the community worship three times a day. A visitor had then but to show himself upon the path leading to Father Bede's hut and invariably the occupant would give him his time and a listening ear. The role of guru was one which Father Bede had tried to avoid, in the belief that there was a place for the spiritual teacher but not for the position of power that accompanied it, but an ashram was traditionally a place where people gathered round a guru to share in his spiritual experience, and the mould of guru was one frequently thrust upon him. Over Easter the visitors came and went in large numbers and it was not for anyone else to speculate as to what it was they took away with them.

I, for my part, had gone there more as an observer than a participant – or so I told myself. As the days passed I learnt something about the simplification of my life which extended beyond coming to terms with the insects and rodents that shared my room, washing my laundry in a bucket of cold water and drying it over a bush, adapting to the lack of photocopying machines and the unavailability of batteries for my tape recorder, and adjusting to sitting cross-legged on the floor to eat my meals out of a tin bowl with one hand. I had arrived with uneasy feelings about the many travellers who came from the West, changed into Indian clothes and adopted an Indian way of living, often to catastrophic effect. It is rare for a European woman to be able to wear a sari with the grace and dignity of the humblest Indian. Rarer still for westerners to be able to use their fingers to eat Indian food with poise. The meeting of East and West was not, I felt, to be effected by such means or at such a level, and even at a more profound level surely the point about the study of eastern experience from a western perspective was not that an absorption in Eastern thought should mean a negation of the West but rather a discovery of the West's buried and defaced spiritual identity, an awakening to those parts of our western past that had been denied us. Mealtimes at the ashram at first did little to dispel such a view. Nor did it really change with time. It was more a question of perspective: my own awkwardness and that of my companions ceased to preoccupy me along with a multitude of other trivial concerns. I discovered a newfound tolerance not entirely unrelated to detachment. Soon the rhythm of the daily prayer and of the Indian music that had at first seemed alien and almost sinister ceased to jar. It had penetrated deep within me and was no longer strange but understood. One morning as I sat watching a vast red sun rise over the mile-wide river bed of the Cauvery and listened to a flautist saluting the dawn, in the extraordinary beauty of the moment the knowledge that the player of the flute was mentally ill no longer seemed of relevance. I was at one with the slight figure standing in the middle of the almost dry river bed mustering all the ability he had, in reverence for the miracle that was taking place on the eastern horizon, and I felt I understood something of the value of the ashram.

By now there were half a dozen brothers who had taken vows and were at various stages of their commitment to the religious life. For those who came seeking to become permanent members of the community there were three stages of commitment to the life of the ashram. The first of these was that of *sadhaka*, 'seeker' or aspirant. The second was that of *brahmachari* or one who had committed himself to the search for God but who need not remain permanently attached to the ashram. Of these there were a growing number in Europe and elsewhere. The third stage was that of *sannyasi*, one who, although in accordance with Indian traditions not bound to remain permanently in the ashram but free to wander elsewhere as the Spirit might lead him, had made a final and total dedication. To him in a ceremony on the banks of the River Cauvery the *kavi* habit was given. Stepping down into the water, the new *sannyasi* would remove his old clothes and allow them to drift away as a symbol of total renunciation and assume the saffron robes, witnessed by the sun, the water and the guru on the bank.

Watching Father Bede as he accompanied others to meditate beside the Cauvery at dawn, or spoke to the assembled congregations without notes but with extraordinary fluency, or as he sat among his brothers in the temple at nightfall, beating out the rhythm of the *bhajans* on an Indian finger drum, there was no escaping the importance of the presence of that 'guru'. This form of worship worked at Shantivanam, one Indian brother confided, because of the relatively small numbers and because it was supported by Father Bede's conviction and his life. That life, he went on, was an inspiration to the community, an ideal to which the brothers could aspire, but his charism was given to him by God. What had been given to him had become for his followers a kind of duty: 'He has long legs and long shoes and it is very difficult to fill them.'

Father Bede no longer milked the cows or cleared thorn-bushes or worked the sun-baked ground. Now he claimed to do nothing with his hands but bless people, but when he did so he felt 'a kind of energy' pass through them. And there was growth all around him. Standing beside a small hut in the ashram's four-acre field, to which he used at one time to escape once a week for a day of quiet retreat, but which he rarely visited now because of the demands of the many visitors, Father Bede surveyed the rich promise of maize and groundnuts before him: 'It's very curious. What is happening here is in a vague way what I wanted from the very beginning, even when I was in the Cotswolds. The idea of a self-supporting community was always there.' In his old age the object of his youthful aspirations had been granted him but in the interim years he had learnt a sometimes difficult lesson, the unreserved surrender to the love of God: 'You cannot will things to happen for yourself. You have to let them happen. One thing I have learnt is not to organize or to attempt to force things. You can make the plans but you must be ready to give them up.'

In another respect also his life seemed to have come full cycle, or perhaps it was that the need for his message had never really diminished. In a way what he was up against now was what he had been up against in the days when Dryden and Pope had stood for all that he disliked: the 'whole rational system'. Now, however, that whole rational system appeared to him to be crumbling. The only point at which, in all our conversations I had glimpsed in Father Bede a glimmer of uncertainty, was with reference to this collapse. 'I don't know where I am,' he acknowledged. Yet he looked out upon the contemporary world with unwavering faith for he saw in it a wealth of initially diverse movements ultimately destined to converge. There were the holistic movement, the eco-logical movement and the feminine movement. It was of vital importance that people discovered the feminine in their lives and linked to this was the peace movement for in a world driven on by the masculine, dominating energy, conflict was inevitable. Only the rediscovery of the feminine could bring peace. There was a movement towards the recognition of sexuality in spiritual life, the acknowledgement that celibacy was a particular calling but that marriage, the union of the masculine and the feminine, was the usual and a valid way to God. There were numerous other separate but interrelated movements, not least of them the movement towards community (and Father Bede saw the future as lying much more with mixed communities), which must inevitably come together: 'So there is a Christian vision which is also a world movement but in order to be able to see this we have to be able to see Christ in this context.'

In *An Indian Benedictine Ashram* Fathers Monchanin and Le Saux had expressed the hope that Saccidananda would one day be one of a number of ashrams with a common basis. Some years later a cardinal representing the Pope at the oriental seminar of 1969 suggested that the future of Christianity in India might rest with small communities of between three and six people scattered throughout the country. It was a vision that was very much Father Bede's ideal. He would like to see Saccidananda Ashram become a mother house from which groups would go forth in twos and threes to form the centre of another sphere. He had come to a holistic view of the universe which recognized the importance of relating to nature and to the world around, to a human community and then to the spirit within, and the value of ashrams in contemporary life was to him as centres where this total human experience could be brought to birth. The aim was to create a human community in harmony with its environment and open to God, God in a very wide sense as revealed in different religious traditions. The original Christian community, the one he had so long ago sought to emulate, was one of total equality and sharing. On the ashram an attempt could be made to break down the hierarchical system in the religious life and in the Church to create a community of equality, sharing and openness. The complexity of such a task did not elude him. It was not simply a question of mixing religions or mixing people, but a very deep awareness of the movement of the Spirit led to openness in all these different ways.

Father Bede had admitted to me that he supposed he was more sensitive now than he had been as a younger man. Even now he had not experienced close contact with extremes of violence, brutality or physical suffering. His, it seemed to me, had been a very different if no less valid calling from that of those who tended the dying in the world's slums, a calling more suited to his own particular abilities. Yet he acknowledged that with every passing day he became more aware of the extent of human suffering. I had seen the demands the anguish, the psychological suffering and confusion of the ever-present visitors made upon him and I had been present in the temple when prayers were offered daily for the victims of the world's disasters, but the question had to be asked: was it not easier to live the ideals of the ashram in an environment of such great natural beauty to which the world for which it was intended as a model came, but only in measured doses? In a sense it was once more the issue of the Himalayan cave or the congested confusion of the noisy, overcrowded temple where it was not unknown for acts of brutality to take place. 'I think', responded Father Bede, 'that you have to create these centres because people cannot live without them.' Like the visitors who came to the ashram most of the brothers brought with them a very deep sense of the conflict in the world. Before people could go out into situations of pain they needed to discover themselves, to find an inner peace and reality, to be very deeply prepared. The ashram could provide a place for such preparation. Ultimately Father Bede, inspired by the work of the Taizé fraternities, would like to see some of the brothers going out from the quiet centre into places of extreme poverty, pain and distress. 'But all this is rather dreaming,' he concluded. 'We are still a very small community.' For the moment he would be content in the conviction that enough had been established to suggest that what had been inititated would continue.

Two encounters loom large in my memory of the long haul back to England. The first was with a Hindu, a fellow passenger on the flight from Tiruchirappalli to Madras who, without prompting, took from his briefcase a notebook and proceeded to explain to me with great kindness and patience what the difference between *Dvaita* and *Advaita* meant to him. The second was again with a fellow passenger, this time on the stretch between Bombay and London. Over breakfast it emerged that he was a German who traded in human hair. I had noticed the barber's shops frequently found on the approach to Hindu temples and I knew that often Hindu women would have their hair cut off and offered to one of the gods in an act of supreme self-sacrifice, but I had never previously considered what the ultimate destination of that hair might be. My German friend was able to enlighten me. The temple Brahmins were quick to retrieve the best quality hair to sell to European businessmen for consumer products in the West. Such an outcome did nothing, I recognized, to detract from the devotion of the women who had surrendered their most prized possession but in the grey chill that followed a disturbed night I could not help but recall some words of Sri Aurobindo pointed out to me in the library at Saccidananda Ashram by the Swiss companion of my journey there. 'The way that humanity deals with an ideal', the sage of Pondicherry had written, 'is to be satisfied with it as an aspiration which is for the most part left only as an aspiration, accepted only as a partial influence.' I found myself wondering whether I had not fallen under the spell of Father Bede's life of ideals put into practice and of his capacity to see the good, wondering whether in fact for every devout self-sacrificing Hindu there was not another prepared to compromise himself and others for financial ends, and whether for every westerner who travelled eastwards in search of an experience of God there was not one whose motives were purely self-interest and commercial gain. Perhaps I should write more of the ambivalence that embraced even the sense of the sacred, but I could not. For I had loved India and India, or at least India as I had perceived it, had somehow swallowed me up and often, on my return, as I drove through the streets of some vast western city, it would seem to me that I was no longer there but in an Indian village bazaar where children laughed, where life was in abundance and God was not in his heaven but everywhere apparent in the world; and often, if only for a fleeting moment, I would recover the deep reality and the silence of the ashram.

Bibliography

Works by Bede Griffiths

The Golden String. Harvill Press 1954, Fontana 1964.
Christian Ashram. Darton, Longman & Todd 1966. Published in the USA as *Christ in India*, 1967.
Vedanta and Christian Faith. Dawn Horse Press 1973.
'Experience of God and the External World in Asian Religions', lecture published in *Cistercian Studies* nos. 2 & 3, 1974.
Return to the Centre. Collins 1976, Fount 1978.
The Marriage of East and West. Collins 1982, Fount 1983.
The Cosmic Revelation. Templegate Publishers 1983, Asian Trading Corporation 1983.

Works by other authors

Capra, Fritjof, *The Tao of Physics*. Fontana 1976.
—, *The Turning Point*. Fontana 1983.
Monchanin, J. and Le Saux, H., *An Indian Benedictine Ashram*. Shantivanam 1951; revised edition published as *A Benedictine Ashram* 1964.
Sheldrake, Rupert, *A New Science of Life*. Blond 1985.
Wilber, K., *The Spectrum of Consciousness*. Quest Books 1979.
—, *The Atman Project*. Quest Books 1980.
—, *Up from Eden*. Routledge 1983.

Index

Index